TEACHING BASIC SKILLS IN READING

TEACHING BASIC SKILLS IN READING

By

LESLIE ANNE PERRY, Ph.D.

Lafayette County Schools
Oxford, Mississippi

and

CYNTHIA C. WOODINGTON, Ph.D.

University of Mississippi
University, Mississippi

CHARLES C THOMAS • PUBLISHER
Springfield • Illinois • U.S.A.

Published and Distributed Throughout the World by

CHARLES C THOMAS • PUBLISHER
2600 South First Street
Springfield, Illinois 62717

ISBN 0-398-05091-0

Library of Congress Catalog Card Number: 84-16316

With THOMAS BOOKS *careful attention is given to all details of manufacturing and design. It is the Publisher's desire to present books that are satisfactory as to their physical qualities and artistic possibilities and appropriate for their particular use.* THOMAS BOOKS *will be true to those laws of quality that assure a good name and good will.*

Printed in the United States of America
Q-R-3

Library of Congress Cataloging in Publication Data

Perry, Leslie Anne.
Teaching basic skills in reading.

Bibliography: p.
Includes index.
1. Reading. 2. Reading--Teacher training.
I. Woodington, Cynthia Coleman. II. Title.
LB1050.P42 1985 428.4'07 84-16316
ISBN 0-398-05091-0

To our husbands, Timothy and James

PREFACE

TEACHING BASIC SKILLS IN READING is designed for use as a textbook in college and university reading education courses. The book can also serve as a resource for reading teachers, reading supervisors, and other school personnel involved in reading instruction. In writing this book, the authors have drawn from the recent experience they both have had as reading teachers and college instructors.

Teaching Basic Skills in Reading is divided into seven chapters. Chapter 1, "Reading Instruction—Past and Present," examines how reading has been taught in the past and how it is currently being taught.

Chapters 2 through 4 encompass the basic word recognition skills. Chapter 2 outlines the teaching of sight words; Chapter 3 examines phonics; and Chapter 4 provides an overview of context usage, structural analysis, and dictionary usage.

Comprehension skills are discussed in Chapter 5 and reading/study skills are presented in Chapter 6. The final chapter of the book looks at ways of developing reading interests and an appreciation of reading. While most reading instruction is carried out on the elementary school level, secondary teachers will find this book contains a great deal of information that they can apply to their teaching situations.

As an aid to the reader, each chapter begins with a pretest and concludes with a posttest. Additionally, Chapters 2 through 6 each contain an "Applications Section" that allows the reader to apply the skills presented in those chapters. To further aid the reader, the authors have placed all key terms in italics when they are first introduced.

No concise method exists for referring to a person whose sex is not indicated. Therefore, to avoid the awkward phrase *he or she* (and the use of plurals when a plural is not indicated), the authors refer to a teacher as *she* and to a student as *he*. Hopefully, this usage will not offend anyone.

L.A.P.
C.C.W.

CONTENTS

TEACHING
BASIC SKILLS
IN READING

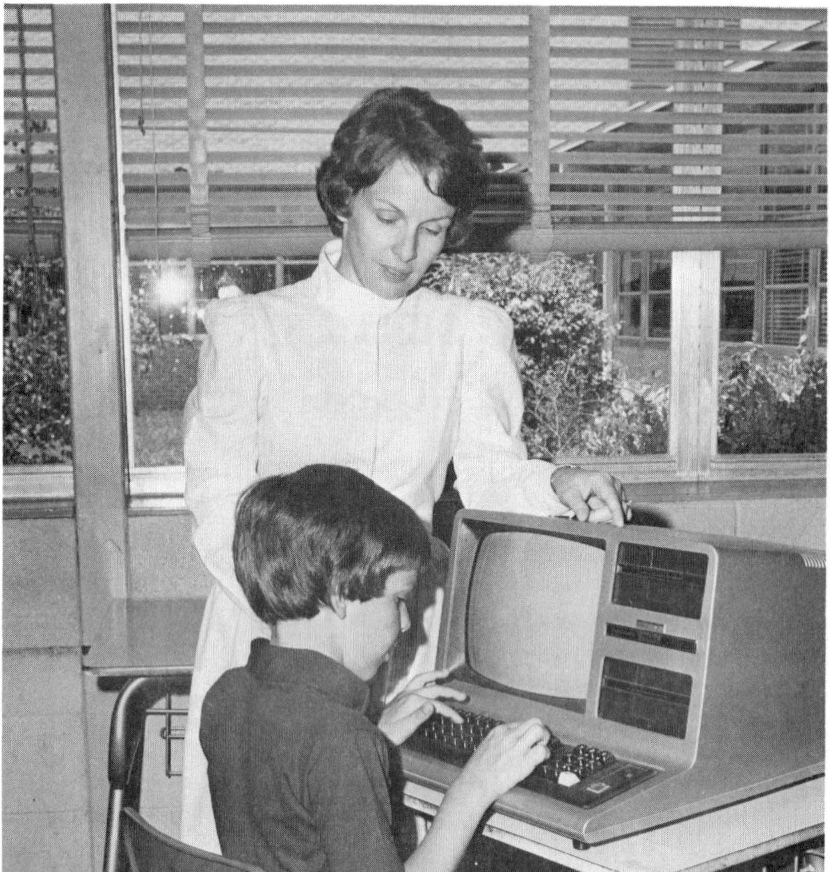

CHAPTER 1

READING INSTRUCTION— PAST AND PRESENT

THIS book is designed to be used as a textbook for college-level courses on teaching basic skills in reading. Its primary emphasis is on basic reading skills. To fully understand these basic skills, one must have knowledge of how reading has been taught in the past as well as how it is currently being taught. Therefore, Chapter 1 contains a brief overview of reading instruction which will provide readers with a background for the remaining chapters.

To enable readers to assess their prior knowledge of the topics presented, Chapter 1 begins with a pretest.

PRETEST

1. What was the first reading textbook published in America?

2. Is there a *best way* to teach reading?
3. What is the primary purpose of reading instruction?
4. Why was reading instruction considered important by the early colonists?
5. Which method did Horace Mann advocate for teaching children to read?
6. How is the *language experience approach* used to teach reading?
7. What *innovations* characterized reading instruction between 1900 and 1930?
8. How did the *Old Satan Deluder Act* influence education?
9. What book, published in 1955, caused the public to become concerned about how reading was being taught in the schools? Which approach to reading instruction did that book advocate?
10. How did most American children learn to read in the 1930s, 1940s, and 1950s?
11. What was a *hornbook*?
12. How was the *alphabet method* used to teach reading?
13. What is the *basal reader approach*?
14. What were the primary features of the *McGuffey Readers*?
15. How do children learn to read through the *individualized* approach?
16. What was the common name for the *American Spelling Book*, published by Noah Webster?
17. For what purpose have *competency testing programs* been mandated by some states?
18. Which approach is currently the most widely used to teach reading?

READING INSTRUCTION THROUGH THE YEARS

The purpose of reading instruction is to develop reading skills in children. Children must develop adequate reading skills if they are to become independent readers. First, children need to be taught word recognition skills to enable them to identify words they encounter in their reading. At the same time that children are taught to recognize words, they must be taught comprehension skills so that they can understand what they read. Children also need to learn reading/study skills if they are to be successful readers in the various content area subjects. Finally, children of all ages need to develop an interest in and appreciation of reading.

As one reads the following sections, one should keep in mind that the purpose of reading instruction is the development of reading skills. This portion of Chapter 1 examines reading instruction in America prior to the twentieth century as well as reading instruction from 1900 to the mid 1980s.

Reading Instruction Prior to the Twentieth Century[1]

In the American colonies, the Bible was often used for reading instruction. Children were taught to read the Bible by the adults who knew how to read. In 1647, the *Old Satan Deluder Act* called for schools to be established in Massachusetts so that the colonial children could learn to read the Bible and avoid Satan. Thus, learning to read was considered worthwhile only because it enabled one to read the Bible.

The New England Primer was the first reading textbook published in America. It appeared around 1690 and was compiled by Benjamin Harris. The book, which reflected the religious emphasis of the colonial period, taught children the alphabet through the use of short rhymes. Learning the alphabet was the first step of learning to read by the *alphabet method.* After the colonial children learned the alphabet, they learned short syllables. Next, the syllables were combined to form words. Finally, children were taught to read these words in phrases and sentences. Youngsters were taught to spell a word at the same time they were taught to read it.

Another reading material used for reading instruction in colonial America was the hornbook. The hornbook was not really a book but was a small, paddle-shaped board that a child could wear on a string around his neck. A piece of paper attached to the board contained the alphabet, common syllables, and the Lord's Prayer. A thin layer of cow's horn was placed over the paper to prevent smudges from little fingers.[2]

---

[1]This section is based on Woodington, C.C. and Perry, L.A.: *Teaching the Reading Teachers* (Springfield, Thomas, 1983), pp. 3-5.

[2]The practice of protecting written materials from finger marks is still in evidence today. Many teachers preserve frequently handled materials with transparent laminating film or adhesive plastic.

In the period following the American Revolution, people began to value reading for purposes other than to read the Bible. It was believed that a literate citizenry could help strengthen the newly independent country. A popular book that appeared in the late 1700s was *The American Spelling Book*, published by Noah Webster in 1798. The book was commonly called the *Blue-back Speller* due to its blue cover. It should be noted that the system of phonics developed in Webster's book was intended more as a means to standardize American speech than as an approach to reading instruction.[3] However, millions of children learned to read and spell phonetically by using the *Blue-back Speller*.

A very popular book series, *The McGuffey Readers* by William Holmes McGuffey, first appeared in 1836. This graded series consisted of a primer and six other books. These books featured *controlled vocabularies*. Thus, only a selected number of words were included in each book. These words were repeated frequently to enable children to learn them. Another notable feature of the series was the type of stories the books contained. Most of the stories were very moralistic and emphasized moralistic *lessons* for the children to learn. By 1920, approximately 122 million copies of these books had been sold. By the late 1970s, sales had reached more than 270 million copies, including copies of revised editions of the books.

In 1837, Horace Mann became the secretary of the Massachusetts State Board of Education. In the twelve years that he held that position, he issued annual reports that influenced teaching methods used in American schools. In 1840, Mann visited European schools that emphasized the *word method* as the primary means for reading instruction. Upon his return to the United States, Mann advocated the use of the word method as a replacement for the variety of phonics approaches in use.

The word method, as advocated by Mann, dominated American reading instruction until the 1890s. Then, once again, phonics was considered the most effective approach. With the *new* phonics, children were taught the sounds of the letters of the alphabet before they were taught to read actual words.[4]

---

[3]Emans, R.: History of phonics. *Elementary English*, *45*: 603, 1968.

[4]Smith, N.B.: *Reading Instruction for Today's Children* (Englewood Cliffs: Prentice-Hall, 1963), p. 192.

Reading Instruction from 1900 to the Mid 1980s

The early 1900s saw the beginning of the educational measurement movement in the United States. For the first time standardized tests were developed that enabled teachers to measure the reading achievement of their students. Also, during this time reading professionals began to advocate silent reading. Previously, most reading in schools was done orally.[5]

During the 1920s, individual differences in reading achievement were first taken into account. Additionally, remedial reading instruction was initiated to provide extra help for children who had difficulty learning to read.[6] The idea of reading readiness also came into being in the 1920s. Prior to that time, formal reading instruction was routinely begun at the same time for all children in a first-grade class and no effort was made to determine which children were *ready* to learn to read.

Another characteristic of reading instruction in the 1920s was the deemphasis on phonics. Silent reading was predominant and phonics was considered taboo. However, some teachers reported that they continued to teach phonics during that time but had a child posted as a *lookout*. The child, who was seated near a window, could signal the teacher if a supervisor arrived so that phonics materials could quickly be hidden.[7]

Between 1930 and 1960 most children learned to read from a basal reader series. These readers featured controlled vocabularies and contained stories to which most children could easily relate. During this period, children were often grouped for reading instruction and most reading was done silently. New words were usually taught *by sight* and phonics and structural analysis were taught after the children learned to read a selected number of words.[8]

During the 1950s, the public became very concerned about how reading was being taught in the schools. Part of this concern resulted from the publication in 1955 of *Why Johnny Can't Read* by Rudolf

[5]Smith, N.B.: What have we accomplished in reading? . . . a review of the past fifty years. *Elementary English, 38*: 141-142, 1961.

[6]Ibid., pp. 142-144.

[7]Ribovich, J.K.: Teaching reading fifty years ago. *The Reading Teacher, 31*: 372, 1978.

[8]Based on Chall, J.S.: *Learning to Read: The Great Debate* (New York: McGraw-Hill, 1967), pp. 13-15.

Flesch. This book strongly recommended a phonics approach for reading instruction.

In the 1960s, the federal government funded a number of studies to determine if there was a *best way* to teach reading. After conducting twenty-seven separate studies, it was concluded that no one approach is superior to all others for beginning reading instruction. Children can successfully learn to read through the use of a variety of methods and materials. Researchers further concluded that the use of a combination of approaches appeared to be superior to the use of a single approach.[9]

During the 1970s and the early 1980s, the majority of the basal reader series used in schools were *eclectic*. These series provided for instruction and practice in all the basic reading skills needed by children and did not place undue emphasis on one particular skill. Additionally, a wealth of interesting and motivating reading materials were available that could be used to supplement or replace a basal reader series.

PRESENT-DAY READING INSTRUCTION

The previous sections provided a brief overview of how reading has been taught from colonial times until the mid 1980s. Information on how reading was taught in the past gives a teacher insight into the common practices and problems connected with reading instruction. However, it is essential that a teacher also be knowledgeable about how reading instruction is carried out in American schools today. Therefore, the following sections present an overview of the characteristics of reading instruction in the mid 1980s as well as a description of the major teaching methods currently in use.

Characteristics of Reading Instruction in the Mid 1980s

Reading instruction in the mid 1980s cannot be characterized by any one teaching method. As with the previous decade, most commercially available reading series are now eclectic and attempt to

[9]Bond, G.I. and Dykstra, R.: The cooperative research program in first-grade reading instruction. *Reading Research Quarterly*, *2*:122-123, 1967.

teach all the reading skills needed by students.

Teachers in the eighties have more information to guide their teaching than did teachers in the past. More attention is directed toward the individual child and how he learns. Most reading teachers of today attempt to help all students reach their potential. These efforts involve starting each student at a reading level where he is able to function and then assisting him in meeting appropriate reading goals. Frequently involved is a plan of early intervention for a child for whom there is an indication that he may have difficulty learning to read. At most schools, specialized personnel are available to which classroom teachers can refer students they feel might need extra help to overcome their reading difficulties.

The 1980s are a time when school reading instruction is frequently subject to criticism by persons and agencies outside of the school. Increased public concern over the teaching of reading and other essential skills has resulted in a number of *competency testing programs* mandated by state legislatures. The purpose of these programs is to prevent students from graduating from high school until they have attained a specified level of proficiency in reading, math, and other areas. Educators and parents are well aware that a student who completes high school and is unable to read will be handicapped throughout life.

Major Methods Currently Used to Teach Reading

A variety of methods or approaches to teaching reading exist today. However, most of these can be classified under one of the three approaches discussed below: basal reader approach, individualized approach, and language experience approach.

Basal Reader Approach

The basal reader approach is the most widely used approach in America today. Over 90 percent of the reading teachers utilize a basal reader series to teach reading to their students.

A few basal series place a great deal of emphasis on learning phonics, while others may stress learning words mainly by sight. However, *most* of the basals available today provide a balanced approach to teaching reading and offer instruction in all necessary skills.

An outstanding feature of basal readers is their provision for sequential skill development. Reading skills are introduced at an appropriate level and are reinforced throughout the series. The *scope and sequence chart* that accompanies most basals can be used by a teacher to determine (1) which skills have already been taught, (2) which skills she is expected to teach, and (3) which skills will be taught at successive levels.

Another advantage of basal readers is the wealth of supplementary materials that are coordinated with these series. These materials can be used by teachers to introduce or reinforce reading skills needed by their students.

Most teachers who use a basal reader series incorporate some type of grouping of students. This practice allows a teacher to place students in a group with other students who read on the same reading level and who have similar needs. These reading groups *rotate* during the time allotted for reading instruction. Reading group rotation is accomplished through careful planning by the teacher. Each day while she is working directly with one group of students she is indirectly managing worthwhile reading-related activities for the remaining two or more groups.

Individualized Approach

Some teachers utilize an individualized approach to teaching reading. This approach allows students to choose their own reading materials and read at their own pace. For this approach, a large number of trade books (library books) are needed. These books must cover a wide range of reading levels and interests so that all students will be able to make appropriate reading selections.

The individualized approach incorporates teacher-student conferences. These conferences, usually held twice a week, allow the teacher to monitor the progress of her students. She can ask them questions about the books they are reading and allow them to read selected portions orally. Also, during the conferences the teacher can make note of any skills she feels that the students need to develop. Then she can work in a small group with the students who have similar needs. Occasionally, through the individual conferences, a teacher will learn that almost all her students need to work on a particular skill. For example, she may find that most of them do not know that *kn* and *gn* at the beginning of words both have the sound of the letter *n*. She may then choose to work with the entire class on those particular sounds.

The individualized approach is not recommended for use in grade one. Students must learn *how* to read before they can read independently. However, once a student has mastered enough reading skills to enable him to read a variety of materials, he may benefit from an individualized reading program. This approach is particularly suited to students in the upper elementary grades.

Language Experience Approach

The language experience approach to teaching reading utilizes stories dictated by the students. After students dictate a particular story to their teacher, they then learn to read it. The approach is highly motivating because students are reading stories that they have helped to write.

One distinct advantage of the language experience approach is that it capitalizes on the relationship between reading and language. This approach utilizes words already in the speaking vocabularies of the students and thus makes reading a successful experience. However, since the stories do contain only those words in the students' oral language vocabularies, this approach is not recommended for students above second or third grade. Older students must begin to learn words not already familiar to them if they are to successfully read the books required for various school subjects.

A teacher using the language experience approach can take selected elements of the dictated stories and use them to teach specific skills. For example, a teacher who wished to teach the sound of the *sl* blend could pull from the stories words that begin with that blend. She could write the words on the chalkboard and guide the children to discover the sound made by the *sl* blend.

In addition to stories dictated by the whole class, students can dictate stories individually. These stories can be kept in personal notebooks. Later, the students can write their own stories to add to their notebooks and can also share their stories with their classmates.

POSTTEST

1. Explain the purpose of reading instruction.
2. What was the purpose of the Old Satan Deluder Act?
3. Identify the original reason for providing reading instruction in the American colonies.
4. Around 1690, the first reading textbook was published in America. What was it called?
5. Describe the *alphabet method* used in colonial America.
6. Elaborate on the format and use of *hornbooks*.
7. The *American Spelling Book* was better known by what name?
8. Describe the *McGuffey Readers*.
9. What instructional method did Horace Mann recommend as a replacement for phonics?
10. Review the *innovations* in reading instruction that were initiated between 1900 and 1930.
11. Between 1930 and 1960, how did most children learn to read?
12. What was the name of Rudolf Flesch's book published in 1955? What approach to teaching reading did the book recommend?
13. Summarize the results of the twenty-seven studies funded by the federal government in the 1960s.
14. Why have some states begun *competency testing programs* in reading and other skill areas?
15. What approach to teaching reading is used by more than 90 percent of America's teachers?
16. Describe the *basal reader approach*.
17. Summarize the features of the *individualized approach* to teaching reading.
18. Evaluate the *language experience approach*.

apartment

CHAPTER 2

SIGHT WORDS

A Word Recognition Skill

THE skills presented in Chapters 2-4 are *word recognition skills*. These skills are sometimes referred to as *word attack skills*. Sight words are discussed in Chapter 2 and phonics in Chapter 3. In

Chapter 4, context usage, structural analysis, and dictionary usage are presented.

The purpose of Chapters 3-4 is to make certain that the readers attain sufficient mastery of the skills discussed in those chapters so that they can teach the skills to their students. In Chapter 2, however, the emphasis is different. The reader will be informed about how to select essential sight words. Additionally, information is provided that will help the reader visualize how sight word instruction can be implemented in the classroom.

The following *sight word pretest* can be used by the reader to assess his/her knowledge of teaching sight words to children.

SIGHT WORD PRETEST

1. What are *sight words*?
2. How is *conceptual framework* related to sight word acquisition?
3. What is the best source of sight words for a teacher using the *basal reader approach*?
4. How can teachers use holidays and other *special occasions* to expand their students' sight vocabularies?
5. What is a *high frequency word*?
6. Why is it important for *content-area* teachers to teach key words as sight words?
7. What are the five *word recognition skills*?
8. How can *language experience stories* be used to teach sight words?
9. Where can a teacher locate high frequency words to teach her students?
10. What is *whole-word methodology*?
11. How should a teacher introduce new words to children?
12. What is a *word bank*?
13. Of what use are *picture dictionaries* for sight word acquisition?
14. How can *peer tutoring* be utilized for sight word drill?
15. In what way can teacher-created stories be used to teach sight words?
16. Why do some teachers label objects around their classrooms?
17. How can spelling, handwriting, and creative writing lessons be used for sight word reinforcement?
18. Why are nouns considered easier for children to learn to read?

19. What is a child's *meaning vocabulary*?
20. In what way can attention to *configuration* clues cause confusion for children?
21. How does *wide reading* build sight vocabularies?
22. Why are *irregular words* taught as sight words?
23. What problems can result from a child having a limited sight vocabulary?
24. When introducing new words, should a teacher write them in manuscript or cursive? Why?
25. For sight word instruction, what is the advantage of teacher-made materials over those that are commercially produced?
26. What should be a teacher's main goal in sight word instruction?
27. How can a child's sight vocabulary help him learn phonics?
28. Why is sight word instruction especially important for children who have just begun reading?

DEFINITION AND IMPORTANCE OF SIGHT WORDS

Sight words are words that a child can recognize without the use of any other word recognition skill. The primary goal of this word recognition skill is to teach a large number of words that the child can recognize *by sight*. The remaining word recognition skills are used by the child when he meets unknown words (words not in his *sight vocabulary*).

Whole-word methodology is an approach for teaching reading that places a great deal of emphasis on teaching sight words and very little emphasis on teaching other word recognition skills such as phonics. This sight word approach is sometimes called the *look-say method*.

The teaching of sight words is related to all approaches to teaching reading. Regardless of how efficient a child becomes in the use of other word recognition skills, he must also possess a large sight word vocabulary if he is to become a proficient reader. Words he can easily *sound out* should eventually become part of his sight vocabulary. Reading would be a very slow process if all readers had to sound out each word they encounter.

Although reading is not actual reading without comprehension, a child must be able to recognize the words before he can comprehend the author's message. Therefore, learning sight words is particularly important for beginning readers. They have not yet attained sufficient knowledge of phonics and structural analysis to enable them to *decode* all the words they need in their reading.

If a child is taught some basic words before he is introduced to phonics, he can apply *phonic generalizations* to known words. This technique enhances learning, for it provides the child with a concrete foundation on which to base future learning. For example, a child who can identify the word *hat* will more readily grasp the short *a* generalization than will a child who cannot identify any words containing the short *a* sound.

The motivational aspect of first teaching the beginning reader basic sight words should not be overlooked. A child who knows some sight words and who has been taught to make use of *context clues* can immediately begin to read simple materials. Early successful experiences with reading are necessary if the child is to have a *good feeling* about reading. Additionally, instruction in other word recognition skills is more meaningful if the child is already reading.

Many words in the English language are *irregular*. These words do not sound the way their letters would indicate they should sound. They must be taught as sight words since children cannot sound them out.

Many irregular words are also *high frequency*. High frequency words are words that occur repeatedly in written English. Since children will encounter high frequency words so often in their reading, they will be at a great disadvantage if they have not learned these words by sight.

The primary cause of reading failure is a child's inability to recognize words. The child who has difficulty with reading usually has a limited sight vocabulary and lacks sufficient knowledge of other word recognition skills. His difficulty with comprehension often stems from problems with word recognition. Furthermore, a child whose sight vocabulary is too limited to allow him to read at an appropriate reading level often will develop a negative attitude toward reading.

The author was recently talking with one of her students who had a negative attitude toward reading. He had been retained in first grade and, at the beginning of his second year in school, knew virtually *no* words by sight and had no word attack skills. On that particular day he had just finished counting the words in his word box. These were words he had recently mastered. His face lit up and he proudly announced, "I used to couldn't read but now I can read!"[1]

LEARNING SIGHT WORDS

As was previously mentioned, the development of a sight vocabulary will be treated differently from the other word recognition skills. For sight words, no rules exist as do for phonics and structural analysis. Once the reader has learned what a sight word is, he/she has *mastered* the skill. Therefore, attention can be turned to learning more about how this very important aspect of word recognition can be developed. In this section the reader will learn various principles of sight word instruction and explore several important sources of sight words.

Principles of Sight Word Instruction

Various procedures or steps can be used to introduce new words to children. The manuals that accompany basal reader series usually contain some suggested procedures for teaching sight words. Many teachers introduce new words to children by using steps similar to the following: (1) Write a sentence on the chalkboard that contains the new word and underline the new word. (2) Read the sentence for the children. (3) Point to the new word and say it aloud. (4) Have the children repeat the new word several times. (5) Have the children spell the word orally and then say the word again. (6) If desired, have the children write the word while they are looking at it and then write it from memory.

As suggested in the steps above, when a new word is introduced to children it should be presented in a *meaningful context*. In other words, it should be introduced in a sentence that the children can easily read if the new word is identified for them. Later, drill can be provided with the word in isolation so that the children can develop

[1]It should be noted that while his attitude had improved greatly, he still had his *bad days* when his earlier negative feelings toward reading reappeared. (Translated, this means he wasn't as rotten as he had previously been.)

instant recognition of the word. This procedure will enable them to more quickly identify the word in other contexts.

When a teacher introduces a new word to a child, it is helpful if she points out distinctive features of the word such as the initial and final letters. This process will help the child learn to recognize the word. However, a teacher should not place much emphasis on the *configuration* or shape of the word since many words have similar configurations. A child who is taught to recognize a word solely by its configuration is likely to confuse the word with other words that have a similar appearance. For example, a child who was taught to recognize the work *book* by noting the two tall letters and the two *o's* in the middle may confuse the word with *hook* or *look*. Therefore, most reading professionals do not recommend the practice of illustrating a word's configuration by drawing a line around the shape of the word.

A teacher may find that children can learn a new word more quickly if, when the word is introduced, it is written in *manuscript* (printing) rather than *cursive*. Manuscript writing permits the children to note the distinctive features of words.

When introducing new vocabulary words, a teacher should present only a few at one time. Children can more easily master a small number of new words. The introduction of too many words in one lesson may result in fewer words being retained.

Some children lack necessary experiences that enable them to understand new words introduced in school. Words in their *oral* (speaking) vocabularies or their *aural* (listening) vocabularies are easier for children to learn to read than are words that are totally unfamiliar to them. Some children need to be provided with background experiences that will help them develop their listening and speaking vocabularies. Additionally, children may need help in developing concepts for words they already use in speaking. Many children use words when speaking that they do not thoroughly understand. For example, the author was recently told the following by one of her students: "I've been sick. My temperature was up to 108 degrees, but it went down to 29 degrees. So I'm okay now."

In the upper elementary grades, childen with well-developed oral language skills will still encounter words beyond their realms of experience. Teachers can use a variety of aids to fill in these gaps and provide their students with a *conceptual framework* for learning new words. The following sources may be utilized to provide a background for a particular reading selection and the new words contained therein: films, filmstrips, slides, transparencies, flat pictures, books, records, audiotapes, videotapes, models, and real objects. When feasible, field trips and resource persons can also be valuable.

Teachers must be as concerned about teaching word meaning as they are about teaching word recognition. One often encounters the term *meaning vocabulary* in educational literature. A child's meaning vocabulary consists of the words he can read and *understand*. A child who can read a word but who does not know its meaning is merely *word calling*. In other words, a child's sight vocabulary should also be his meaning vocabulary.

Children can more easily learn words that are of interest to them. Nouns are easier for children to mentally *picture* than are other parts of speech. For example, most children can more quickly form a mental image to correspond with the word *helicopter* than they can for the word *when*.

Finally, teachers must provide practice in sight word recognition through the use of a variety of activities that are both interesting and motivating to students. Lengthy drills should be avoided, as several short drill sessions are usually more effective than one long session.

Sources of Sight Words

From the foregoing discussion one should surmise that the authors strongly recommend that students be given ample opportunities to develop extensive sight word vocabularies. The questions that come to mind are, "What words will I teach as sight words?" and "Where do I locate lists of essential words?" The following sections present information on the primary sources of words for sight word instruction.

Basal Reader Vocabulary

As was noted in Chapter 1, the number of elementary teachers using a basal reader is probably in excess of 90 percent. Teachers who do use a basal reader series should consider the words in that basal the most important ones for their students to learn.

Obviously, a child cannot read the stories in his reader if he does not know the words. A child who has a great deal of difficulty in a particular reader more than likely did not master the words at the previous level(s). Assuming that the child is placed at an appropriate level in his basal reader series, a teacher can reduce vocabulary deficiencies by reviewing the words he has forgotten.

Words introduced at each level of a basal series are usually listed in the back of the students' books and/or in the teacher's manuals. These lists are useful to a teacher, in that she can see which words are taught at previous and subsequent levels, as well as which words she must teach.

High Frequency Word Lists

As was mentioned earlier, there are some words that occur so frequently in the English language that children need to recognize them quickly. Many of these *high frequency words* are irregular and cannot be *sounded out*. Therefore, teachers often teach words from various high frequency word lists.

Many of the words on high frequency word lists are also the words taught in basal reader series. Some of the words, however, are not always found in basal readers and teachers can add these to the words they teach from their basal. As these lists are readily available and include many necessary words, remedial reading teachers, and teachers who do not use a basal, find them to be essential sources of sight words.

Three of the many available lists of high frequency words are discussed below. One of the lists, The Instant Words by Edward Fry, is reproduced in its entirety at the end of this chapter.

DOLCH LIST.[2] The Dolch list consists of 220 words that are frequently found in books written for children in the primary grades (grades 1-3). It originally appeared in 1936 but is still considered useful today. An updated version (arranged according to reading levels) is widely available for use by teachers. Also available is a list of ninety-five nouns to be used in conjunction with the 220 words on the Dolch list. The author has found, however, that the use of nouns that are meaningful to her own students makes reading much more interesting for them.

[2]Dolch, E.W.: A basic sight vocabulary. *Elementary School Journal*, 36:456-460, 1936.

THE INSTANT WORDS.[3] This list contains 300 words that students are likely to encounter in all types of reading (see Appendix). These words make up around 65 percent of all written English. The first 100 words alone make up around 50 percent. And the first ten words account for about 24 percent of all written materials!

Included with this list are several suffixes to be used by the teacher to form common variations of these words. The arrangement of the words is according to the frequency of their occurrence in a variety of written materials (textbooks, library books, and magazines). This listing is a good source of words needed by readers of all ages.[4]

KUCERA-FRANCIS LIST.[5] One thousand high frequency words are contained in the Kucera-Francis list. The words are listed according to frequency of occurrence and are taken from all types of written materials. Teachers at the intermediate, junior high, and secondary levels will find that this list is a source of words that have a high utility value for their students in all areas of study.

Words Encountered in Language Experience Stories

Chapter 1 contained a discussion of the language experience approach to teaching reading. In that approach, students learn to read stories that they have dictated to the teacher. Teachers who use a basal reader series can still use certain aspects of this method. For example, stories dictated by the students can be used to reinforce new words and skills introduced in the basal.

Language experience stories are a good source of words for students to learn by sight. These dictated stories contain words that are already in the speaking vocabularies of the students. Therefore, they are words to which the students can easily *relate*.

If a teacher utilizes *word banks* (see "Word Banks" in a later section) and has the children place words in their *banks* in alphabetical order, many worthwhile activities can evolve. One such activity

[3]Fry, E.: The new instant word list. *The Reading Teacher*, 34:284-289, 1980.

[4]In the school system where the author teaches, these words were selected as the ones to be mastered by remedial reading students in grades four through six. They have also been taught to students in grades three and seven. The author highly recommends this list of sight words.

[5]Kucera, H., and Francis, W.N.: *Computational Analysis of Present-Day American English* (Providence: Brown University, 1967).

would be for the children to use the words from their banks in creative writing. They can select the words from their word banks as they need them in their writing.

Words Encountered in Other Situations

Teachers should not overlook the many opportunities that occur throughout the school day to expand the sight vocabularies of their students. The opportunities may occur incidentally, during content-area reading, or during individualized reading.

In most classrooms, various situations routinely occur that allow students to expand their sight vocabularies almost without effort. Words that pertain to an upcoming event, words that pertain to seasons and holidays, and various other *special occasion words* can easily be taught as sight words. For example, words like *valentine, heart, Cupid, president*, and *country* could be taught in February. The presentation of a play at school could provide a meaningful opportunity to teach words like *stage, props, narrator*, and *costumes*.

Content-area subjects like science, social studies, English, and math involve many words that are new to students. Often, these new words are not ones that students use in their everyday speech. Therefore, a teacher must make a special effort to teach all key words in these subjects as sight words. Unless the students can successfully read the material, their understanding of the subject matter will be very limited at best.

APPLICATION OF SIGHT WORD USAGE

By completing the following exercises, the reader can apply some of the concepts presented thus far in Chapter 2.

1. Give four examples of *irregular* words.
2. Indicate which three of the following words would be easiest for students to learn.

   a. Halloween b. that c. of
   d. with e. dinosaur f. school
3. What word list might a first- or second-grade teacher find useful?
4. According to Edward Fry's word list, what are the ten most fre-

quently used words in written English?

5. What percent of written English is comprised of these ten words?
6. Based on past experience, speculate on which is the most frequently used word in *spoken* English.
7. Write a paragraph that incorporates the first ten words of *The Instant Words*.
8. Name six *special occasion words* that a teacher might teach during the month of December.

CLASSROOM APPLICATIONS

As was noted earlier, students who have a great deal of difficulty with reading often have very limited sight vocabularies. Frequently, they do not know enough words to enable them to read and comprehend most written materials. More than likely, sufficient practice was not provided at previous levels. To enable these students to learn new words, a great deal of practice is necessary.

Teachers must use a variety of techniques to provide their students with activities that assure the necessary repetition of sight words. Teacher's manuals contain numerous suggestions for teaching sight words. Many of these suggestions can be used for teaching the words initially or for providing necessary reinforcement. Several types of instructional techniques a teacher can use to teach and reinforce sight words are presented below.

Teaching Words from Basal Readers and Word Lists

After sight words from a basal reader series or a high frequency word list are introduced to students, some of the following types of activities can be used to provide reinforcement.

Games and Activities

Games and other activities should focus on words that the students need to learn. Commercial games are available for sight word practice. However, teachers often find that materials they make themselves are better suited to the needs of their students. Teacher-made materials can reinforce words specifically chosen by the teacher. Whereas commercially prepared materials are not likely to include all the words taught in the classroom.

A particularly useful teacher-made instructional item is a multi-purpose game board that can serve as the basis for a variety of sight word activities. These activities can be used to provide children with necessary practice on words encountered in the classroom. However, word games that students will play without teacher assistance should contain only words that have been previously introduced. The author has found that children are highly motivated by activities based on game boards when small, plastic characters from a movie or television series are used as the manipulative game parts.

Another useful classroom technique to reinforce sight words is *peer tutoring*. This technique pairs a student who knows the words with a student who does not. Peer tutoring can be utilized to help pupils who need additional drill on words already introduced.

Bulletin boards can also be used to reinforce sight words students need to learn. For example, a bulletin board could be based on an outer space theme with words printed on space ships, stars, and planets. As with game boards, bulletin boards should be designed so that they can be used with various sets of words.

A teacher must remember that different children may react differently to the same activity. Careful thought must be given to the possible outcomes of all activities such as the above-mentioned bulletin boards. The author recalls an incident that resulted from the use of a bulletin board in her classroom. Each child made a paper bird with his name on it. The bulletin board featured a tall pole that supported a paper birdhouse. Paper perches were on either side of the pole and a picture of a cat was near the bottom of the pole. For each word a child correctly pronounced, his bird was moved up to the next higher perch. All was going well (so the teacher thought) until a parent called one evening to say that his child had been crying since he got home from school. The child was afraid the cat was going to get his bird! Needless to say, the author discontinued the use of that particular bulletin board. When the author reflected upon the activity, she realized that the underlying purpose of the activity was worthwhile but that the cat was apparently too threatening to some children.

Creating Stories

One successful technique that the author frequently uses is that of creating stories that contain words from the basal reader series. These stories are written about television characters that are of interest to the students. To determine the characters used in the stories, an *interest inventory* should be administered at the beginning of the school year. This inventory can include items that will allow the teacher to discover her students' favorite television programs.

The author has found that students have little difficulty learning to read the names of their favorite television characters. The children become so excited about reading the stories that they do not realize they are being drilled on the words from their basal. It should be noted that words from high frequency word lists can be reinforced by the same technique. Furthermore, the use of the students' own name in the stories greatly increases their appeal.

Using Selected Words for Spelling and Writing Lessons

Teachers often select words for spelling lessons that they want their students to learn to read. If a child can spell a word, he will certainly have no difficulty reading it each time it is encountered. Words for spelling lessons can come from the basal reader or word lists.

Teaching *word families* as spelling words is an excellent method for expanding a student's sight vocabulary and making him aware of spelling and sound patterns in words. Word families are comprised of words that contain similar endings. If a child masters one word in such a family he can readily learn others. For example, a child who knows the word *cat* can easily be taught the words *bat* and *rat*.

Handwriting lessons can be another avenue for sight word reinforcement. By writing these words students will be forced to note the distinctive features of each of them.

For students who are capable of writing stories independently, creative writing activities can evolve around words to be taught by sight. Creative writings are those which a student composes on his own. The content is limited only by the student's imagination.

Word Banks

Many teachers have their students develop individual *word banks*.

These banks are actually boxes that contain cards on which words have been printed. Some teachers allow a child to place a word in his bank only after he has mastered the word. Whereas, other teachers prefer to use a word bank that is divided into two sections. One section contains words the student has learned and the other section contains words he needs to work on.

The authors strongly disagree as to the *best way* to use word banks. However, either of the above-mentioned methods will allow a student to visualize the progress he is making toward increasing his sight word vocabulary. Both methods allow for continued practice of learned words so that the student will not forget the words he has mastered.

With the latter approach, the teacher can print an unknown word on one side of the card and a sentence containing the word on the reverse side. The student must correctly pronounce the word on three separate occasions to indicate mastery. With each correct identification, the student places a check mark on the card. When he has three checkmarks, he is permitted to place the word in the section of his word bank that contains previously learned words.

Word banks can motivate students to learn new words when other techniques may fail. Most students are thrilled when they count their word cards and discover that they have learned many new words. To a young child, the cards are almost like money in the bank!

Teaching Additional Words

As noted throughout this chapter, students need many opportunities to expand their sight vocabularies. Not all sight word instruction has to result from the planned reading program. Much incidental learning can occur. The following sections contain suggestions that allow students to learn words in addition to those from the basal reader and word lists.

Labeling

Teachers in the primary grades often label various objects and areas in their classrooms. As a child sees these words day after day he will eventually learn the words by sight. For example, a child who sees the word *door* each day will associate that word with the object.

When he later sees that word in a sentence, he will be able to recognize and correctly identify it.

For children in kindergarten or first grade, a teacher can make a second set of labels and have the children match the words with the ones they see around the room. Various learning activities can be used to expand a child's use of these new words.

A calendar and helpers chart are commonly found in many primary classrooms. Both are excellent sources of words that can become a part of the children's sight vocabularies. Each morning as the teacher talks about the day of the week, etc., she can call attention to the distinctive features of the words involved.

Language Experience Stories

As was previously mentioned, language experience stories are a good source of sight words. Through the use of these stories teachers can highlight words that are abstract and irregular (e.g. *there*) but are in the speaking vocabularies of the students. The author has experienced much success using a modification of this approach. After the students have read a selection in the basal, they sometimes retell the story in their own words. The author records their thoughts on the chalkboard or on a chart tablet so that the students can immediately read the story they have dictated.

Language experience stories can also be written on duplicating masters. If done, each student should have two copies of the story he has helped to write. One copy can be read by the student in class for immediate reinforcement of the sight vocabulary. The other copy can be placed in the student's individual reading notebook for future independent reading.

Picture Dictionaries

Students in grades one and two can greatly benefit from using a picture dictionary. The dictionaries contain numerous pictures with the word that names each picture printed under it. Students can immediately associate the pictured item with its corresponding printed label. In addition to possibly acquiring some beginning dictionary skills, students can learn numerous words by sight.

The uniqueness of picture dictionaries motivates most children.

They particularly enjoy using a picture dictionary for independent learning activities. One type of learning activity that utilizes picture dictionaries has the student look for words that contain like-phonic elements. They might search for words that begin with an *st* blend or words that contain a short *a* sound. They can then make a list of the words they found and share the list with classmates.

Wide Reading

"Children learn to read by reading" is a statement frequently heard by most teachers. No substitute exists for wide reading at a child's independent level. Materials written at this level are those which a child can read and comprehend without teacher assistance. Furthermore, a large stock of books, magazines, and other written materials should be readily available to all students to encourage frequent reading.

Through wide, independent reading a child repeatedly meets words in a variety of contexts. As he continues to read widely, the new words he encounters are added to his sight vocabulary.

A child reading in an individualized reading program will learn new words primarily through his independent reading. Moreover, children in all types of reading programs can benefit from wide reading. The opportunity to read a variety of reading materials helps a child see *what reading is* and helps him learn to enjoy reading.

SIGHT WORD POSTTEST

1. Identify the five *word recognition skills*.
2. Define *sight word*.
3. What is the primary goal in sight word instruction?
4. What is another term for *whole-word methodology*?
5. Why is sight word instruction particularly important for beginning readers?
6. How can knowledge of some basic sight words aid a child in learning phonics?
7. Why must *irregular words* be taught as sight words?
8. What is the advantage of teaching *high frequency words* by sight?

9. Identify two problems that might result from a child having a limited sight vocabulary.
10. Describe a procedure that can be used to introduce new words to students.
11. Why should teachers avoid the practice of drawing boxes around words to illustrate their *configurations*?
12. What is the advantage of writing new words in manuscript rather than cursive?
13. Why is it sometimes necessary for teachers to provide their students with a *conceptual framework* for learning new words?
14. Explain why a child's sight vocabulary should also be his *meaning vocabulary*.
15. Why can a child more readily learn to read nouns than words that function as other parts of speech?
16. From what source should teachers who use basal readers select words to teach their students?
17. Explain why *The Instant Words* by Edward Fry is a good source of sight words. Identify and describe two other useful word lists.
18. What feature of *language experience stories* makes them a good source of words to teach to students?
19. Why should key words in *content-area subjects* be taught as sight words?
20. How can *special occasions* be used to build sight vocabularies?
21. Why are teacher-made materials sometimes better for teaching sight words than materials that are produced commercially?
22. How can *peer tutoring* be useful for sight word drill?
23. Describe how a teacher might use *created stories* for sight word reinforcement.
24. What is the advantage of using sight words in spelling and writing lessons?
25. In what way can *word banks* motivate students to learn new words?
26. For what purpose are labels often placed on classroom objects?
27. How can *picture dictionaries* help young children learn sight words?
28. Describe how a child can build his sight vocabulary through *wide reading*.

Appendix

THE INSTANT WORDS

by Edward Fry

(Used by Permission)

First Hundred (common suffixes *s, ing, ed*):

First 25 Group 1a	Second 25 Group 1b	Third 25 Group 1c	Fourth 25 Group 1d
the	or	will	number
of	one	up	no
and	had	other	way
a	by	about	could
to	word	out	people
in	but	many	my
is	not	then	than
you	what	them	first
that	all	these	water
it	were	so	been
he	we	some	call
was	when	her	who
for	your	would	oil
on	can	make	now
are	said	like	find
as	there	him	long
with	use	into	down
his	an	time	day
they	each	has	did
I	which	look	get
at	she	two	come
be	do	more	made
this	how	write	may
have	their	go	part
from	if	see	over

Second Hundred (common suffixes *s, ing, ed, er, ly, est*):

First 25 Group 2a	Second 25 Group 2b	Third 25 Group 2c	Fourth 25 Group 2d
new	great	put	kind
sound	where	end	hand
take	help	does	picture
only	through	another	again
little	much	well	change
work	before	large	off
know	line	must	play
place	right	big	spell
year	too	even	air
live	mean	such	away
me	old	because	animal
back	any	turn	house
give	same	here	point
most	tell	why	page
very	boy	ask	letter
after	follow	went	mother
thing	came	men	answer
our	want	read	found
just	show	need	study
name	also	land	still
good	around	different	learn
sentence	form	home	should
man	three	us	America
think	small	move	world
say	set	try	high

Third Hundred (common suffixes *s, ing, ed, er, ly, est*):

First 25 Group 3a	Second 25 Group 3b	Third 25 Group 3c	Fourth 25 Group 3d
every	left	until	idea
near	don't	children	enough
add	few	side	ear

food	while	feet	face
between	along	car	watch
own	might	mile	far
below	close	night	Indian
country	something	walk	real
plant	seem	white	almost
last	next	sea	let
school	hard	began	above
father	open	grow	girl
keep	example	took	sometimes
tree	begin	river	mountain
never	life	four	cut
start	always	carry	young
city	those	state	talk
earth	both	once	soon
eye	paper	book	list
light	together	hear	song
thought	got	stop	leave
head	group	without	family
under	often	second	body
story	run	late	music
saw	important	miss	color

8 eight
10 ten
Mm Nn Oo Pp Qq Rr Ss Tt Uu Vv Ww Xx Yy Zz
Scholastic Phonics Chart
Digraphs and Blends

CHAPTER 3

PHONICS

A Word Recognition Skill

THE five word recognition skills discussed in Chapters 2-4 complement each other and can all be useful aids for students. Phonics, when taught with other word recognition skills, can help prepare students to become successful, independent readers.

Teachers cannot teach a skill that they do not thoroughly understand. It is the purpose of this chapter to make certain that teachers attain sufficient mastery of phonics so that they can teach phonic analysis to their students. The content is presented in a manner that will enable individuals with no prior knowledge of phonics to comprehend this important chapter.

The following *phonics pretest* can help the reader determine how much he/she already knows about phonics.

PHONICS PRETEST

1. Which are easier for children to learn, *consonant sounds or vowel sounds*? Why?
2. What three major letter patterns indicate a *long vowel sound*?
3. What is *phonics*?
4. Does the principle of the closed syllable indicate a *long vowel* or *short vowel* sound?
5. What is a *schwa sound*?
6. How does *phonics* differ from *phonetics*?
7. In what way can teaching *initial consonant sounds* in isolation cause later problems for children?
8. When a *y* occurs at the end of a word or syllable, does it function as a *vowel* or a *consonant*? What sounds can it have?
9. What is a *phoneme*? What is a *grapheme*? What is meant by *phoneme/grapheme relationships*?
10. In what way can students' names be used to teach phonics?
11. What is the difference between a *voiced* and *voiceless th*?
12. Which approach, *inductive* or *deductive*, allows students to *discover* phonic generalizations?
13. What is the relationship of *visual discrimination* and *auditory discrimination* to phonics instruction?
14. How does the *analytic approach* to phonic analysis differ from the *synthetic approach*?
15. What is a *diphthong*?
16. What are three letter patterns that indicate *silent initial consonants*?
17. What is a *consonant blend*? What is a *consonant digraph*?
18. How are *phonograms* used for *initial consonant substitution*?
19. What are *r-controlled vowels*?
20. Why is it considered a good practice to use familiar words to illustrate new phonic generalizations to students?

DEFINITION AND IMPORTANCE OF PHONICS

Phonics is the study or use of sound and symbol relationships. Phonics differs from *phonetics* which is the study of speech sounds. Many sources refer to a spoken sound as a *phoneme* and to a written symbol or letter as a *grapheme*. Using those terms, phonics is the study or use of *phoneme/grapheme relationships*.

When a reader uses *phonic analysis*, he examines an unknown word to determine the sounds represented by the individual letters or letter combinations. He then blends the sounds together to form (or pronounce) the word. Finally, he must rely on the context of the passage to verify the accuracy of his analysis.

Phonics has its roots in the *code approach* of the past. The code approach required that children first learn the letters of the alphabet. They then learned common syllables and, finally, words, phrases, and sentences.

Before phonic generalizations can be applied to words of more than one syllable, children must learn how to break words into syllables. Knowledge of phonics can be very helpful to children when they meet these unknown *multisyllabic* words or when they meet unknown words of only one syllable. In fact, knowledge of beginning consonant sounds, when used with clues provided by the reading passage, is often all a reader needs to help him determine an unknown word.

The primary purpose for teaching phonics is to enable children to become independent readers. Children must learn how to deal with words they do not immediately recognize. Children who possess enough skill with phonics that they can decode most unknown words will not have to rely on a teacher or other adult to pronounce the words for them.

LEARNING PHONICS

The following sections contain a discussion of various aspects of phonics and phonics instruction. The content of phonic analysis is presented first to provide teachers with a background that will enable them to better understand subsequent sections.

Content of Phonic Analysis

As was mentioned earlier, reading teachers cannot successfully teach phonics unless they are familiar with all aspects of the skill. The following *generalizations* are those most frequently needed by students at all levels. These selected generalizations have a higher utility value than many other phonic generalizations; thus, they have fewer exceptions. Some generalizations are designed to account for exceptions to other generalizations. However, not all exceptions can be taken into consideration. As was stated in Chapter 2, many words simply cannot be *sounded out* and must be taught as sight words.

The sequence for teaching phonic generalizations is usually determined by the type of reading program a teacher uses. Teachers using a basal reader program can follow the instructional sequence outlined in the series. A *scope and sequence chart* accompanies most reading series. The chart shows the concepts to be developed at each level.

Consonant sounds are easier for students to learn because they are more consistent (have fewer variations) than do vowel sounds. However, a teacher would not teach all consonant generalizations before teaching any that pertain to vowels. The generalizations presented below are divided into consonant and vowel generaliations as an aid to the reader. It should be noted that this listing does not represent a recommended sequence for teaching phonics to children.

The generalizations presented in the following sections may include more phonics skills than some children need. Conversely, there will be some children who are interested in learning additional generalizations. Teachers should adapt their instruction to meet the needs and interests of their students. Other sources can be consulted for lesser-used phonic generalizations.

Consonant Generalizations[1]

1. Most *consonants* have one sound. They generally have the same sound in the *initial* and *final* positions of words (beginning and ending positions). For example, the letter *b* has the same sound in the words *bath* and *tub*.

---

[1]Based on generalizations in Woodington, C.C. and Perry, L.A.: *Teaching the Reading Teachers* (Springfield: Thomas, 1983), pp. 15-16.

2. Two *consonants* that consistently have more than one sound are the letters *c* and *g*. They both have a *hard* and *soft* sound. The hard *c* and *g* are the sounds one usually associates with these letters. This sound is heard when the *c* or *g* is followed by *a, o,* or *u*. Examples are these:

   hard *c* as in *cat, cot, cut*
   hard *g* as in *gas, got, gum*

   The soft *c* is the sound usually associated with the letter *s*, and the soft *g* is the sound associated with the letter *j*. These soft sounds are heard when the *c* or *g* is followed by *e, i,* or *y*. Examples are these:

   soft *c* as in *cent, city, cycle*
   soft *g* as in *gem, giant, gym*

3. *Consonant blends* (also called clusters) are two or three adjacent letters that are pronounced together but still can be heard separately. There are several types of blends:

   a. Initial consonant blends in which the letter *s* is the first consonant:

   sc as in *scare*
   sk as in *skunk*
   sm as in *smell*
   sn as in *snake*
   sp as in *spin*
   st as in *stop*
   sw as in *swift*
   spr as in *sprout*
   str as in *strong*

   b. Initial consonant blends in which the letter *l* is the second or third letter:

   bl as in *blimp*
   cl as in *close*
   fl as in *flop*
   gl as in *glare*
   pl as in *plane*
   sl as in *slide*
   spl as in *splash*

   c. Initial consonant blends in which the letter *r* is the second or third letter:

   br as in *broom*
   cr as in *creep*
   dr as in *drip*
   fr as in *fruit*
   gr as in *gripe*
   pr as in *price*
   tr as in *trick*
   scr as in *scrape*
   spr as in *spring*
   str as in *stripe*

   d. Initial consonant blends in which the letter *w* is the second letter:

dw as in *dwarf* — *sw* as in *sweep*
tw as in *twin*

e. Final consonant blends (blends that occur at the end of words):

st as in *rust* — *sk* as in *task*
ld as in *mold* — *mp* as in *damp*
nd as in *sand*

4. *Consonant digraphs* are two adjacent letters that make a single sound, unlike either of the two consonants. Consonant digraphs can occur as follows:

a. Initial consonant digraphs:

ch as in *chip* — *ph* as in *phone*
sh as in *shop* — *voiced th*[2] as in *that*
voiceless th as in *think* — *wh* as in *wheel*

b. Final consonant digraphs:

ch as in *much* — *gh* as in *laugh*
ph as in *graph* — *sh* as in *hush*
th as in *bath*

5. *Silent consonants* can occur in words. Some of the more common silent consonants are:

silent *g* of *gn* as in *gnat* — silent *k* of *kn* as in *knee*
silent *w* of *wr* as in *wrist* — silent *gh* after *i* as in *high*

Vowel Generalizations

1. *Short vowels*. The five *vowels (a, e, i, o. u)* usually have short sounds in the medial (middle) position of words. This generalization is often called the principle of the *closed syllable* or the consonant, vowel, consonant generalization (CVC). Examples are these:

short *as* as in *hat* — short *e* as in *pet*
short *i* as in *dig* — short *o* as in *top*
short *u* as in *bug*

If there is no beginning consonant, as in the case of a vowel, consonant pattern (VC), the vowel is still short. Examples are these:

---

[2]When a person pronounces the *voiced th* his vocal chords vibrate. The vocal chords do not vibrate when the *voiceless th* is pronounced.

short *a* as in *at*
short *e* as in *Ed*
short *i* as in *it*
short *o* as in *odd*
short *u* as in *up*

2. *Long vowels*. The five *vowels (a, e, i, o, u)* can have long sounds, or say their own names, in three major letter patterns.[3] These patterns illustrate the long vowel sounds:

a. When two vowels are adjacent, they form a vowel digraph. Usually the first vowel is long and the second vowel is silent (CVVC or VVC pattern). Examples are these:

long *a* as in *mail*
long *e* as in *eat*[4]
long *e* as in *feet*
long *o* as in *coat*

b. When a medial or initial vowel is followed by a consonant and final *e*, the medial vowel usually has a long sound and the final *e* is silent (VC final *e*, or VCV pattern). Examples are these:

long *a* as in *cake*
long *e* as in *Pete*
long *i* as in *ice*
long *o* as in *rope*
long *u* as in *cube*

c. When a vowel occurs at the end of a word or syllable, it usually has a long sound (CV pattern). This generalization is called the principle of the *open syllable*. Examples are these:

long *e* as in *me*
long *o* as in *go*

d. Sometimes vowels have the long sound when followed by certain letters. The most common are these:

long *a* of *ay* as in *pay*[5]
long *i* of *igh* as in *light*
long *i* before *ld* as in *mild*
long *i* before *nd* as in *kind*
long *o* before *ld* as in *old*
long *o* before *lt* as in *bolt*
long *o* before *mb* as in *comb*

3. *Vowels followed by r (r-controlled)* have neither the long nor short sounds. Usually their pronunciations are these:

---

[3]A long *u* can have two different sounds. It can say its own name in words like *cube* and it can have an o͞o sound in words like *fruit*.

[4]The *ea* digraph is not very consistent. It has several sounds in addition to the long *e* sound.

[5]The *ay* is sometimes considered a vowel digraph. (The *y* functions as a vowel.)

ar as in *barn*
or as in *corn*
er as in *her*
ir as in *dirt*
ur as in *hurt*

4. *The letter a followed by l, ll, u, and w* has neither the long nor short sound. The following examples illustrate its pronunciation:

al as in *walk*
all as in *ball*
au as in *haul*
aw as in *saw*

5. *Schwa sound.* Often vowels in unstressed syllables are softened so that they then make a sound similar to a short *u* sound. This schwa sound is represented by the symbol ə. Examples are these:

*a*round el*e*phant dign*i*ty butt*o*n

6. *Diphthongs* consist of two vowels that occur together and have neither the long nor short sound. When a *y* or a *w* occurs in a diphthong, it functions as a vowel. Illustrations of diphthongs are these:

oi as in *boil*
oy as in *toy*
ou as in *house*
ow as in *cow*[6]

7. When two *o*'s occur together, they have neither the long nor short sound. Their pronunciation can be:

o͞o as in *moon*
o͝o as in *book*

8. The letter *y* functions as a vowel when it is the final letter of a word or syllable. It can have these sounds:

long *e* as in *baby*
long *i* as in *sky*
short *i* a in *bicycle*
silent *y* as in *hay*

Principles of Phonics Instruction

Before young children can benefit from phonics instruction, they must first be able to detect differences in letters and letter sounds. The ability to distinguish between the various *letters* of the alphabet involves *visual discrimination*. The ability to distinguish between various *letter sounds* involves *auditory discrimination*. While children do not have to be able to recognize all the letters of the alphabet before they can learn letter sounds, they must be able to detect likenesses and

[6]In a number of words the *ow* has the long *o* sound *(blow, snow)*. The *ou* can also have the long *o* sound (*dough*).

differences in letters.

Phonic generalizations should not be taught as *rules*. Children should be told that generalizations do not apply to all words but are meant to be used as tools when they encounter unknown words. They should be taught to check the context of the written passage to verify the accuracy of their pronunciation. If it does not *make sense*, they will then need to try an alternate pronunciation. For example, if a child substitutes a short vowel sound where he had incorrectly used a long vowel sound, he may then produce the correct word that both makes sense to him and fits the context of the passage.

The amount of phonics taught will vary with the age, ability, and needs of the students. Beginning readers should be taught only as much phonics as they *need* to help them read the printed materials at their appropriate level. For young children, *less is better*. Only generalizations with very high utility value (very few exceptions) should be taught to beginning readers. Additionally, to avoid confusion, a teacher would not want to point out a large number of exceptions when presenting a new generalization. If students mention exceptions, these exceptions can be acknowledged and can serve to emphasize that phonics is not infallible.

Reading teachers at all levels, not just beginning reading, must possess a thorough knowledge of phonics. Most basal reader programs *introduce* most of the content of phonics in the primary grades (grades 1–3). However, these skills are *maintained* throughout the basal program. At all grade levels, teachers need to help students decode unknown words. It is simply not fair to the students when their teacher is not adequately prepared to teach phonics.

The twenty-six letters of the English alphabet represent approximately forty-two to forty-six sounds. To add to this problem, there exist many regional variations in pronunciation. Most people have had the experience of watching a television program that featured a speaker from a different part of the United States who pronounced his words differently from what the viewer was used to hearing. Phonic generalizations cannot take into account all these regional variations in speech. For example, when the author was teaching in the Middle West, she encountered a phonic generalization in her teacher's manual that she attempted to teach to her students. The manual was obviously written by people in another region of the country, for the generalization was not representative of the speech of her students.[7] When teachers present new phonic generalizations to their students they should use words already familiar to the students as examples of the generalizations. They should also be particularly careful when they select words to be used as examples. These words must be illustrative of the generalization being taught. A teacher who uses the word *sugar* to teach the sound of the consonant *s* will only confuse the students and frustrate herself.[8]

Likewise, teachers must be careful when using commercial materials designed for phonics instruction. The author found several sets of materials in her classroom that were produced by well-known companies but that, if used, would thoroughly confuse even the brightest students. One such set of materials used a picture of a squirrel as an example of the initial *s* sound. A child who learned the *s* sound from that picture might attempt to pronounce the word *sock* as *squ-ock*. Teachers need to be especially careful not to use words containing consonant blends or digraphs to teach single consonant sounds.

Another difficulty with consonant sounds arises when teachers attempt to teach initial consonant sounds in isolation. When initial consonant sounds are taught in isolation without attaching the remainder of the word, their sounds are distorted. For example, if students are taught that the letter *p* sounds like *puh*, they are likely to decode the word *pup* in this manner: *puh-u-puh*. The resulting word is not likely to lead to comprehension of the written passage. Comprehension should always be the end result of phonic analysis.

After students have been taught a particular phonic generalization, they must be given opportunities for sufficient practice. Teacher's manuals and other sources provide suggestions for phonics practice that is both motivating and meaningful. For older students, nonsense words can be used for practice of previously learned generalizations.

Several drawbacks exist regarding phonics instruction. As one

[7] This experience occurred during the author's first year of teaching and she thought that she was supposed to teach everything in the manual. Therefore, it was not without some guilt that she abandoned the attempt to teach that particular generalization.

[8] Similar confusion would result if a teacher used the word *head* to teach letter patterns that indicate a long *e* sound. While the *ea* pattern does represent a long *e* sound in many words, it has the short *e* sound in the word *head*.

can conclude from the foregoing discussion, many different phonic generalizations must be learned to cover all common letter patterns. Many letters simply do not sound the same in all words, and many sounds can be represented by several different letters or letter patterns. Additionally, as mentioned earlier, children can apply phonic generalizations to words of more than one syllable only after they divide the word into syllables. Syllabication skills, considered part of structural analysis, are discussed in Chapter 4.

Another drawback lies not with phonics itself but with the students who use phonic analysis. If a decoded word is not in a student's listening or speaking vocabulary, it will be meaningless to him. The context of a written passage cannot always be relied upon to provide sufficient meaning clues if the unknown word is a word with which the student is not familiar. Furthermore, an overreliance on phonics produces mechanical word-by-word readers.

Types of Phonics Instruction

The type of instruction used by a teacher is in part determined by the type of reading program used. For example, programs may advocate teaching either an analytic or synthetic approach to phonic analysis. Additionally, phonics instruction can be presented either inductively or deductively. A brief discussion of these approaches is presented below to make the reader aware of differences that exist in the types of phonic analysis and in the manner in which phonics can be taught.

Analytic and Synthetic Approaches

The analytic and synthetic approaches are techniques that children are taught to use for phonic analysis. In other words, teachers elect to teach children to use phonics primarily through an analytic or synthetic approach.

ANALYTIC APPROACH. When children use the *analytic approach* they look at a whole word and analyze the word part by part. They note the sounds made by the various phonic elements contained in the word. They then blend the sounds together and pronounce the word (either orally or mentally). Finally, they determine if the decoded word *makes sense* in the context in which it occurred. An illustration of this technique would be when a child encountered the unknown word *lead* in the sentence, "Jay will *lead* the Halloween parade." Using his knowledge of phonics, the child would analyze the unknown word to determine its pronunciation. After decoding the word, he would immediately reread the sentence using his chosen pronunciation to see if it fits the meaning of the sentence. If he found that the decoded word did not make sense in the sentence, he would try an alternate pronunciation.

Advocates of the analytic approach to phonic analysis emphasize that children who use this method tend to enjoy reading more than those who use the *synthetic approach*. Its emphasis on meaning makes learning to read less of a mechanical process.

Synthetic Approach. The *synthetic approach* frequently emphasizes speech sounds in isolation. Students are taught the sounds made by various letters or letter combinations and are then taught to blend those sounds together to form words. The approach usually requires that students look at word parts before considering the word as a unit of meaning. For example, a teacher using this approach might teach the sound of a long *a* in isolation (by itself) rather than in a whole word such as *cake* (or in a phrase such as *a birthday cake*).

While the synthetic approach places less emphasis on reading for meaning, certain aspects of the approach can successfully be used to help children become independent readers. Particularly helpful for beginning readers are initial consonant substitution activities with phonograms (mentioned in a later section of this chapter).

Inductive and Deductive Approaches

The inductive and deductive approaches are techniques or methods a teacher can use to teach children. While these approaches can be used to teach many different concepts to children, they are most often discussed in the context of phonics instruction.

Inductive Approach. The *inductive approach* is a discovery technique. The teacher shows the students several words that contain like-phonic elements. She then leads the students to *discover* the phonic generalization that applies to the words. As an illustration, the teacher could put the words *star, stop*, and *stick* on the chalkboard. The students could be led to discover that they all begin with the *st* consonant blend and they then could determine the sound produced by that blend. This technique enhances learning since the students are actively involved in the learning process.

Students who learn a concept by the inductive approach will be more likely to both retain that learning and transfer it to other situations. On the other hand, students who are merely told about a particular concept are less likely to retain and transfer their knowledge. However, the inductive approach can be time consuming and it is not always practical for all learning to take place in this manner.

Deductive Approach. A teacher who uses the *deductive approach* simply states a phonic generalization and expects the students to automatically apply it when they meet unknown words. Since students often do not thoroughly understand the principle behind the generalization, long-term memory is not likely to occur. Even those students who are repeatedly exposed to a particular generalization and required to commit it to memory are frequently not able to apply the generalization.

APPLICATION OF PHONIC ANALYSIS

The following exercises will enable the reader to apply some of the concepts presented in this chapter.

1. Give four examples of *graphemes*.
2. Which of the following words would *not* be useful as examples of the initial *s* sound?

a. sandbox	b. star	c. sock
d. sink	e. shell	f. square

3. For which of these nonsense words would a *hard sound* for *c* or *g* be indicated?

a. geb	b. coaf	c. gax
d. cip	e. cyple	f. gidaf
g. gopt	h. gybet	i. cak
j. culf	k. gup	l. cebb

4. Of the following words, which contain *consonant blends* and which contain *consonant digraphs*?

a. plate	b. step	c. wheel
d. dress	e. chin	f. shirt
g. skate	h. this	i. smart

5. Indicate whether a *voiced th* or a *voiceless th* is heard in each of

these words.

a. that	b. these	c. thin
d. then	e. thank	f. the

6. List four words that contain *silent initial consonants*.
7. Determine if the *e* in each of the following words is *long, short, silent*, or *r-controlled*.

a. feet	b. shape	c. her
d. jet	e. bean	f. fern
g. Jane	h. me	i. pen

8. Name two words that contain a *schwa sound*.

CLASSROOM APPLICATIONS

While some students read well at their expected reading levels without the aid of much phonics, most students can benefit from some type of phonics instruction. A variety of learning experiences are necessary to enable students to learn and use phonic analysis. As seen below, these learning experiences can be part of a planned sequential phonics program or can occur incidentally.

Sequential Phonics Instruction

Most basal reader programs provide for the sequential introduction and development of phonics skills. With this instruction, skills introduced at one level are usually practiced at subsequent levels. By following the suggested sequence of a basal or other commercial reading program, teachers can be certain that their students are introduced to the elements of phonics required at their level.

A wealth of commercial materials are available to aid the teacher in teaching phonics. However, as with teaching sight words, many teachers prefer to produce their own materials. Teachers who develop some of their own materials often find that the materials they make are better suited to the needs of their students than are materials that are commercially produced.

When a teacher introduces a new element of phonics to young students it is often helpful to show pictures or objects that illustrate the new element. To introduce beginning consonant sounds, the author has frequently used small objects placed in lunch sacks. The letter that stands for the sound to be learned was printed on the front of its corresponding sack. A variety of small objects from the classroom and household were used to fill the sacks. When the children saw a pencil in the sack marked *Pp* they could more easily learn the sound of that letter than if they had simply been told the sound.

Initial consonant substitution is often recommended in the beginning levels of basal readers. After students have learned most of the initial consonants, they *substitute* different consonants at the beginning of a particular word ending. For example, the word *pan* becomes *man* when an *m* is substituted for the *p* and attached to the *an* ending. The word *man* then becomes *can* when a *c* is substituted for *m*. *Final consonant substitution* can be accomplished in a similar manner. The word *can* becomes *cat* when a *t* is substituted for the *n*.

The substitution of medial vowels can follow consonant substitution. As an illustration, the word *cat* above becomes *cot* when the *a* is changed to an *o*. Commonly, chalkboards and worksheets are used for these substitution activities. Moreover, flashcards and other manipulative materials can be made for additional instruction. Manipulative items that students can use independently are especially motivating to young children since they enjoy handling these items.

Word families, or *phonograms*, are groups of words that all have the same ending. Word families can be used for initial consonant substitution activities. The following sets of words are ones the authors have found particularly useful. While the listing is confined to the substitution of single consonants, consonant blends and consonant digraphs can also be used to create new words.

1. Phonograms containing the long and short sounds of *a*
   a. ad: bad, dad, fad, had, lad, mad, pad, sad, Tad
   b. am: bam, ham, jam, Pam, ram, Sam, yam
   c. an: ban, can, Dan, fan, man, Nan, pan, ran, tan, van
   d. ap: cap, lap, map, nap, rap, sap, tap
   e. at: bat, cat, fat, hat, mat, Nat, pat, rat, sat, vat
   f. ade: fade, jade, made, wade
   g. ail: bail, fail, Gail, hail, jail, mail, nail, pail, rail, sail, tail
   h. ain: gain, main, pain, rain
   i. ake: bake, cake, fake, Jake, lake, make, rake, sake, take, wake

   j. ale: bale, Dale,male, pale, sale, tale
   k. ame: dame, fame, game, lame, name, same, tame
   l. ane: cane, mane, pane, sane
   m. ate: date, fate, gate, hate, late, mate, rate
   n. ay: day, Fay, hay, jay, Kay, lay, may, nay, pay, ray, say, way

2. Phonograms containing the long and short sounds of *e*
   a. ed: bed, fed, Jed, led, Ned, red, Ted, wed
   b. eg: beg, keg, leg, Meg, Peg
   c. ell: bell, fell, Nell, sell, tell, well, yell
   d. en: Ben, den, hen, Jen, Ken, men, pen, ten
   e. et: bet, jet, let, met, net, pet, set, wet, yet
   f. ean: bean, dean, Jean, lean, mean
   g. eal: deal, heal, meal, Neal, real, seal, veal
   h. eat: beat, heat, meat, neat, seat
   i. eed: deed, feed, need, seed, weed
   j. eek: meek, peek, seek, week
   k. eel: feel, heel, peel, reel
   l. eep: beep, deep, jeep, keep, peep, weep

3. Phonograms containing the long and short sounds of *i*
   a. id: bid, did, hid, kid, lid, rid, Sid
   b. ig: big, dig, fig, jig, pig, rig, wig
   c. ill: dill, fill, hill, Jill, mill, pill, sill, till, will
   d. im: dim, him, Jim, Kim, rim, Tim
   e. in: bin, fin, kin, pin, tin, win
   f. ip: dip, hip, lip, rip, sip, tip, yip, zip
   g. it: bit, fit, hit, kit, lit, pit, sit, wit
   h. ike: bike, hike, Mike, pike
   i. ile: file, mile, pile, tile
   j. ine: dine, fine, line, mine, nine, pine, tine, vine

4. Phonograms containing the long and short sounds of *o*
   a. ob: Bob, cob, fob, gob, job, lob, mob, rob, sob
   b. op: bop, cop, hop, mop, pop, top
   c. ot: cot, dot, got, hot, jot, lot, not, pot, rot, tot
   d. oat: boat, coat, goat, moat
   e. ole: dole, hole, pole, role, tole
   f. ope: cope, dope, hope, mope

5. Phonograms containing the short *u* sound
   a. ub: bub, cub, hub, nub, pub, rub, sub, tub
   b. ug: bug, dug, hug, jug, lug, mug, pug, rug, tug
   c. ull: dull, gull, hull, lull
   d. um: bum, gum, hum, mum, sum, yum
   e. un: bun, fun, gun, pun, run, sun
   f. ut: but, cut, gut, hut, jut, nut, rut

Incidental Phonics Instruction

Teachers who use a language experience or individualized approach to teach reading will need to offer some type of phonics instruction so that their students will not be deficient in this area. Some teachers prefer to place their students in small groups for phonics instruction. Others prefer to teach phonics to the entire class at one time. However, caution must be exercised to assure that the students see a connection between phonics and reading and do not view phonics as a separate subject.

Teachers who use a basal reader program will find many occasions when phonics can be taught *incidentally*. Students often discover phonic generalizations on their own. Teachers should capitalize on these discoveries even if the generalization has not yet been encountered in the basal reader. Taking advantage of student interest often results in quick mastery of a skill or concept.

The children's own names and the names of objects around the classroom can be used for incidental phonics instruction. For example, if there are students named *Sharon* and *Shawn*, the *sh* digraph can easily be illustrated. Likewise, the names *Charles* and *Chad* could be used to illustrate the *ch* digraph.

Opportunities often occur for teachers of young children to teach or reinforce vowel sounds and the silent *e* principle. As an illustration, the word *cub* becomes *cube* when an *e* is added to the end of the word. While a short *u* is heard in *cub*, a long *u* is heard in *cube*. Other words that can be used in this manner are: *mad, made; pet, Pete; rip, ripe;* and *not, note*. The author has illustrated the silent *e* principle with a set of word cards that have a moveable *e*. The *e* can be raised and the remaining word has a short vowel sound. When the *e* is put back in place, the word has a long vowel sound.

PHONICS POSTTEST

1. Define *phonics*.
2. What is *phonetics*?
3. Define *phoneme*. Define *grapheme*. Explain what is meant by *phoneme/grapheme relationships*.
4. Can a child more easily learn *consonant sounds* or *vowel sounds?* Why?
5. Compare and contrast *consonant blends* and *consonant digraphs*.
6. Describe the difference between a *voiced* and *voiceless th*.
7. Identify three letter patterns that indicate *silent initial consonants*.
8. What type of *vowel sound* is indicated by the principle of the *closed syllable*?
9. Describe three letter patterns that result in a *long vowel sound*.
10. Define the term *r-controlled vowel*.
11. What is a *schwa sound?*
12. What constitutes a *diphthong?*
13. Briefly relate the function and sounds of the letter *y* when it occurs at the end of a word or syllable.
14. How are *auditory discrimination* and *visual discrimination* related to learning phonics?
15. Explain why words already familiar to students should be used to illustrate new phonic generalizations.
16. How can the teaching of *initial consonant sounds* in isolation result in confusion to students?
17. Compare and contrast the *analytic* and *synthetic approaches* to phonic analysis.
18. Describe a procedure a teacher might follow when using the *inductive approach* to teach phonic generalizations.
19. Explain how a teacher would use *phonograms* for *initial consonant substitution* activities.
20. How can students' names be useful for phonics instruction?

YOUR
IN
HEALTH
READING
WEBSTERS
DICTIONARY

CHAPTER 4

CONTEXT USAGE, STRUCTURAL ANALYSIS, AND DICTIONARY USAGE

Word Recognition Skills

CONTEXT USAGE

CONTEXT USAGE PRETEST
DEFINITION AND IMPORTANCE OF CONTEXT USAGE
LEARNING CONTEXT USAGE
- Types of Context Clues
  - Semantic Clues
  - Syntactic Clues
  - Picture Clues
- Principles of Context Usage Instruction

APPLICATION OF CONTEXT USAGE
CLASSROOM APPLICATIONS
CONTEXT USAGE POSTTEST

STRUCTURAL ANALYSIS

STRUCTURAL ANALYSIS PRETEST
DEFINITION AND IMPORTANCE OF STRUCTURAL ANALYSIS
LEARNING STRUCTURAL ANALYSIS
- Content of Structural Analysis
  - Elements of Structural Analysis
  - Syllabication and Accent
- Principles of Structural Analysis Instruction

APPLICATION OF STRUCTURAL ANALYSIS
CLASSROOM APPLICATIONS
STRUCTURAL ANALYSIS POSTTEST

DICTIONARY USAGE

DICTIONARY USAGE PRETEST
DEFINITION AND IMPORTANCE OF DICTIONARY USAGE
LEARNING DICTIONARY USAGE
  Dictionary Strategies
    Locational Strategies
    Pronunciation Strategies
    Meaning Strategies
  Principles of Dictionary Usage Instruction
APPLICATION OF DICTIONARY USAGE
CLASSROOM APPLICATIONS
DICTIONARY USAGE POSTTEST

CHAPTERS 2 and 3 discussed the word recognition skills of sight words and phonics. Chapter 4 presents a discussion of the three remaining word recognition skills: context usage, structural analysis, and dictionary usage.

CONTEXT USAGE

In actual classroom practice, students are usually taught context usage prior to phonic analysis. However, due to the length of the discussion on phonics, the authors presented it in a separate chapter. As was mentioned earlier, the five word recognition skills complement each other and can be developed concurrently. One would not teach the entire content of one area before teaching another skill area.

This portion of Chapter 4 presents a discussion of context usage. As a convenience to the reader, all aspects of context usage are discussed before the introduction of structural analysis and dictionary usage. The following *context usage pretest* will help readers assess their prior knowledge of this word recognition skill.

CONTEXT USAGE PRETEST

1. When is the best time to teach *context usage*?
2. Why can students often recognize a word *in context* but not *in isolation*?
3. What are *semantic context clues*?

4. How might a child's *oral language ability* affect his skill in using context clues?
5. In context usage practice, which is easier for a child to fill, a blank space near the beginning of a sentence or a blank space near the end of a sentence? Why?
6. What are *syntactic context clues*?
7. Why do critics sometimes refer to context usage as a *guessing technique*?
8. How can a book's *illustrations* help a child comprehend the book's message?
9. When a child encounters an unknown word, is it helpful for him to continue reading the rest of the paragraph?
10. In what way can *context usage* help students comprehend words with multiple meanings?
11. How can *picture clues* help children expand their sight word vocabularies?
12. Should teachers ignore children's *miscues* if they are *meaningful substitutions*?

DEFINITION AND IMPORTANCE OF CONTEXT USAGE

Context usage refers to a student's utilization of clues inherent in a written passage or its accompanying illustrations. *Verbal* or *word clues* are provided by the author whereas *picture clues* are created by the illustrator.

The context in which an unknown word appears can be very helpful to a student. The student can make use of surrounding words, phrases, and sentences to help him pronounce and comprehend this unfamiliar word. The surrounding context may help the student recall a previous encounter with the word. This recollection often enables him to pronounce the word and understand its meaning. The student can then reread the sentence or passage to verify the accuracy of his choice.

Context usage can help a student clarify the meaning of many words. In the English language, a number of words have multiple meanings with the correct meaning determined only by the context in which the word appears. In addition to determining word meanings, context can also indicate the pronunciation of many words. For example, the word *record* can be pronounced *re-cord* or *rec-ord*. Each pronunciation denotes a different meaning. The word *read* can also be pronounced two different ways; thus, a student must use the context in which the word appears to determine which pronunciation is correct.

Like verbal or word clues, picture clues can be very useful to children. Most books written for beginning readers contain numerous illustrations. These pictures make the books attractive and appealing to children (and adults). However, illustrations also convey meaning. If a child is confused by a word such as *clown* and can see a clown pictured in the story, he will probably be able to correctly pronounce the word. Eventually the word will become a part of his sight vocabulary, but at the beginning stages of learning to read, a child's sight vocabulary is very limited. Thus, picture clues (and verbal clues) can enable a child to read a book even when he does not know all the words.

Critics will occasionally suggest that the use of picture clues will result in an overdependence on pictures to convey meaning. The author maintains that such is not the case. In the years that she has spent teaching children to read, she has concluded that picture clues are an absolute necessity for young children learning to read. Until students have mastered a story's words by sight, they heavily rely on picture clues. However, once these words are learned, students no longer refer to the story's pictures for meaning clues. Furthermore, the author would not advocate the use of a reading program that does not include pictures at the beginning levels.

Some educators have labeled the use of verbal context clues as a guessing technique. It has been the author's experience that most children can be taught to use the context of a passage to make intelligent decisions in their attempt to recognize unknown words. For example, the author recently overheard one of her students reading a library book aloud. He read: "Little pig, little pig. I *went* to come in." He then corrected himself and read: "Little pig, little pig. I *want* to come in." He was able to correct his own error upon reading the entire sentence because he saw that the context demanded another word in place of the word *went*.

If a teacher analyzes a child's incorrect responses she will usually find that they are based on what the child understands about the meaning and structure of the English language. If a child pronounces a word that differs from the actual word seen printed before him, the word he substitutes usually makes sense in the sentence. For example, if a child does not immediately recognize the noun in a sentence, he might substitute another noun for the unknown word. However, he is not likely to substitute a verb or other part of speech for an unknown noun. He will use a word that *makes sense*. Reading is a meaning-getting process, and context usage is more closely related to meaning-seeking than the other word recognition skills.

Unconsciously, children predict what others will say when speaking. They use the context of the remainder of the spoken sentence to aid them if they hear a word with which they are not familiar. Most children can transfer this *natural* listening skill to the reading task. They can be taught to employ context usage as a quick and efficient aid to word recognition. Context usage is particularly helpful to children who lack phonics and structural analysis skills to help them decode unknown words. However, even for students with advanced decoding skills, context usage is an extremely valuable tool for word recognition.

LEARNING CONTEXT USAGE

From the foregoing discussion the reader may have concluded that context usage is a skill that students can acquire on their own without formal instruction. This conclusion is partially valid. Context usage often does occur almost automatically. However, many children need guidance to help them fully utilize this important word recognition skill.

Teachers need to have a thorough understanding of the various types of context clues and of some basic principles of context usage instruction. Therefore, a discussion of these topics is presented in the following sections.

Types of Context Clues[1]

Earlier in this chapter verbal and picture clues were mentioned.

[1]Based on Woodington, C.C. and Perry, L.A.: *Teaching the Reading Teachers* (Springfield: Thomas, 1983), pp. 13-14, 54.

Verbal context clues can be either *semantic clues* or *syntactic clues*. These two types of clues are often used simultaneously. Semantic and syntactic context clues are discussed in the following sections as are *picture clues*.

Semantic Clues

Semantic clues, as the name implies, refer to meaning. The student searches the remainder of the sentence or passage for clues that might indicate the meaning of the unknown word. A student might encounter a sentence such as, "Tim relaxed in a chair under the shade tree." If the reader did not already know the word *relaxed*, he could probably recognize it by using the clues in the remainder of the sentence.

Semantic clues will assist a student in recognizing only the unknown words that are already in his listening or speaking vocabulary. The student's past experiences and background knowledge of the discussed topic influence the successful use of semantic clues.

Clues to the meaning of an unknown word can occur in several different forms. The following classification[2] illustrates the manner in which semantic clues may occur. In each example, the word in italics is the word designated as *unknown*.

CLASSIFICATION OF SEMANTIC CONTEXT CLUES

1. Comparison or contrast clue:
   Yesterday was sunny, but today is *overcast*.
2. Synonym clue:
   Tyson was *excited* about the trip to the zoo. He was happy.
3. Summary clue:
   The school *custodian* waxed the floor, washed the windows, and cleaned the boards before school started this year.
4. Mood clue:
   The sun was shining, the flowers blooming, the birds were singing, the day was *magnificent*.
5. Definition clue:

[2]Based on McCullough, C.: Context aids in reading. *The Reading Teacher*, 11:227-229, 1958.

The *shrubbery*, bushes, near the house had to be cut.

6. Clue of familiar expression or language experience:

"I can't believe I ate the *whole* thing!"

Syntactic Clues

Syntactic clues are used along with semantic clues to aid a student in recognizing unknown words. Syntactic context clues depend on word order and word function in a sentence. Word order, the position of a word in a sentence, is highly predictable in the English language. Students with an adequate knowledge of language usage can use this predictability to identify unknown words.

Word function refers to the grammatical usage of a word in a sentence and also assists in the identification of an unknown word. A student who does not recognize the word *corduroy* in the sentence "Connie has a new corduroy dress" will probably guess the word functions as an adjective rather than another part of speech.

When a student uses syntactic clues, he anticipates what will come next in a sentence. Even if he does not pronounce the exact word he sees, as long as his substitution fits the context of the sentence, he still can comprehend the author's message. As was noted earlier, comprehension of the author's message is what reading is really about.

Picture Clues

As was mentioned in a previous section, picture clues are those clues found in the illustrations contained in many children's books. Illustrations are particularly useful for young children who are just learning to read. Illustrations not only hold a child's interest but also provide valuable clues to help the child recognize unknown words. Often, when a child is reading and encounters an unknown word, a quick glance at the illustration will enable him to immediately arrive at a pronunciation and meaning for that word.

Picture clues also help expand a child's sight vocabulary. After a child encounters a word several times in a book and uses picture clues to help him recognize the word, he will more than likely *know* the word. By using picture clues, he will have taught himself the word and will be able to recognize it in other contexts as well.

Principles of Context Usage Instruction

Unlike some of the other word recognition skills, there is not a particular content that a student must master for effective context usage. However, some basic principles exist regarding context usage instruction that teachers may find helpful.

As was noted earlier, a student's oral language ability and his background of experiences affect his ability to use context clues. To illustrate, a child who encounters the sentence, "Nancy rode up the escalator at the airport," may have difficulty using context clues to recognize the word *escalator* if he has never seen an escalator.

Activities that expand a child's listening and speaking vocabularies can be extended to include oral practice in context usage. Providing oral practice prior to written practice is a natural sequence, since children learn to speak before they learn to read. Children who have been taught to utilize the context of spoken sentences will be better equipped to utilize the context of written sentences.

Written exercises for context usage instruction often involve sentences with blanks in them. The student is required to fill in the blank with the appropriate word. A blank at the end of a sentence is easier for a child to fill, since there are more clues in front of the space. Conversely, a blank near the beginning of a sentence is more difficult for the child to complete.

When teachers provide students with context usage practice they should always use sentences with meaningful clues. The sentence "Barbara has a ______" is not going to give a child much practice with context usage, since a number of words could go in the blank. If the sentence was followed by a second sentence that contained more clues, it would be useful for context usage practice. For example, the sentences could read, "Barbara has a ______. She has sneezed and had a runny nose all day." These sentences could give a child practice in using surrounding words to determine what should go in the blank. This type of practice makes a child more aware of the context of a passage.

In the preceding example, the word *cold* would be the appropriate word to place in the blank. If a teacher desired to give students practice in using context to identify a difficult, unknown word, these sentences would not be appropriate if the word *cold* was considered the unknown word. The word *sneezed* in the second sentence is more difficult for students to recognize than is the word *cold*. In other words, the written unknown word should be the most difficult word in the sentence. Furthermore, if a passage contains too many unknown words, it would not be useful for practice with context usage because not enough clues would be present.

The author frequently encounters students who cannot recognize certain words in isolation but who can easily read them when they appear in sentences. These students need the context of a sentence to help them recall certain words. Since context usage is such a useful tool, students need to be taught very early that when they meet an unknown word they should continue reading to the end of the sentence. They should then go back to the unknown word to see if they can recognize it. Moreover, students should be taught that clues to the identity of unknown words can be found in surrounding sentences as well. Clues may be found in the sentence before or after the sentence in which the unknown word apears. Occasionally, after an entire paragraph has been read, a student will then be able to recognize a word that occurred near the beginning of the passage.

Some teachers suggest that if a child orally reads a word incorrectly but still retains the meaning of the passage, that this *miscue* should be ignored. Other teachers maintain that the child should always be corrected so that incorrect responses will not be reinforced. Actually, a wise teacher usually ignores some miscues and corrects others as the situation requires. It should be noted that when a child reads silently he is probably making a number of *meaningful substitutions* for unknown words. However, as long as he still comprehends what he reads, this practice should not be a problem.

APPLICATION OF CONTEXT USAGE

To apply some of the concepts presented in this portion of Chapter 4, complete the following exercises.

1. Based on the *Classification of Semantic Context Clues*, determine which type of *semantic context clue* is illustrated by this sentence.

   Tom took his dog to the *veterinarian*, the animal doctor, to get his shots.

2. Indicate the type of *semantic context clue* illustrated by this sentence.

Last year she was sick a lot, but this year she is *healthy*.

3. What type of *semantic context clue* is illustrated by these sentences?

   Lora was *elated* when she opened the present. She was very happy.

4. In which of these sentences might a child more easily identify the underlined word (or make a *meaningful substitution*)?
   a. Connie and Mike went to watch the football *competition*.
   b. Cindy and Jimmy *hesitated* when they saw the bus coming.
5. For which of these sentences would it be easier for a student to supply the missing word?
   a. Kyle got a new soccer ______ for his birthday.
   b. Laura went to the store to buy a ______.
6. Which of the following sentences would be more appropriate to use for context usage practice?
   a. Anne flew on the plane to Arizona to visit her *mother*.
   b. Julie is too big to play with *dolls*.
7. Indicate which sentence (a or b) shows a *meaningful substitution* in the sentence, "The boy came to our house."
   a. The boy come to our house.
   b. The boy cat to our house.
8. Write two sentences containing the word *lead*. Each sentence should incorporate a different meaning and pronunciation of the word.

CLASSROOM APPLICATIONS

Teachers who use a basal reader program will usually find that the program provides for the development of context usage as well as all other word recognition skills. For teachers who wish to provide their students with additional context usage practice, or for teachers who use a language experience or individualized reading program, a number of commercial materials are available.

In addition to using commercial materials, many teachers develop their own exercises to provide their students with context usage practice. For young children who are first learning context usage, the teacher can write sentences on the chalkboard that omit one word or that only provide the first letter of the word. If a teacher provides this beginning consonant (or beginning and ending consonants), the word choice is narrowed considerably. Not many words will begin with that particular letter and also fit the context of the sentence. As an illustration, in the sentence, "David has a round _______," several words could be used to complete the sentence. However, if the sentence read, "David has a round b_______," fewer possibilities exist.

In addition to placing a blank in a sentence, teachers can also provide students with three or four words and have them select the correct word to complete the sentence. A similar activity for older students could utilize their actual reading material (e.g. a story from their basal). When students encounter a difficult word, their teacher can suggest three or four possible *meanings* for the unknown word and the students can select the meaning that can be supported by the context.

Illustrations cut from magazines or catalogs can be used for an activity that helps children make use of context clues. A teacher can write a sentence on the chalkboard, omitting one word and putting a blank in its place. She can then display several pictures and let the students select the picture that illustrates the omitted word. For example, the teacher may write, "Tod put on his _______ and went out to play football." Pictures of a raincoat, a three-piece suit, and a football outfit could be displayed. Children enjoy activities of this nature that allow them to participate and practice a reading skill at the same time.

Teachers should be constantly alert to opportunities that occur on the *spur of the moment* which allow them to spontaneously provide their students with context usage practice. Oral exercises that promote context usage can be used at various times throughout the school day. The author occasionally uses words with which she knows her students are not familiar. She uses the words in a manner that allows the students to determine their meaning from the context in which they occurred. This technique not only helps students learn to make use of oral context clues but expands their listening vocabularies as well.

The above-mentioned activities can all effectively be used to develop context usage by students. However, the author has found that the best time to teach context usage is when a student has the greatest need for the skill. This need occurs when a student actually encounters an unknown word in his reading. The teacher can ask questions that will call the student's attention to the context in which the word occurred. This approach will enable the student to see how truly valuable context usage is as a word recognition tool.

CONTEXT USAGE POSTTEST

1. How can *context usage* help a student when he encounters a word that has several different meanings?
2. Why is context usage much more than a *guessing technique*?
3. Define *semantic context clues*.
4. Define *syntactic context clues*.
5. In what way are *picture clues* used by children?
6. Explain how *picture clues* can help expand a child's sight vocabulary.
7. How is *oral language ability* related to context usage?
8. Is it easier for a child to fill in a blank space at the beginning of a sentence or at the end of a sentence? Why?
9. What causes students to correctly identify a word *in context* but not know the same word when it is presented *in isolation*?
10. Should a child be taught to read the entire passage when he encounters an unknown word? Why?
11. How should a teacher react to a child's *meaningful substitutions*?
12. When can context usage most effectively be taught?

STRUCTURAL ANALYSIS

Thus far, the word recognition skills of sight words, phonics, and context usage have been discussed. This portion of Chapter 4 focuses on structural analysis, which will be followed by a discussion of the fifth and final word recognition skill: dictionary usage.

Prior to reading the structural analysis portion of Chapter 4, the reader should take the *structural analysis pretest*. The pretest will enable the reader to determine how much he/she already knows about structural analysis.

STRUCTURAL ANALYSIS PRETEST

1. What is *structural analysis*?
2. At what grade level can structural analysis be introduced to students?
3. What is a *base word*?
4. What is an *affix*?
5. How do spelling patterns influence the manner in which *plurals* are formed?
6. Which are easier for students to learn, *prefixes* or *suffixes*? Why?
7. What is the *cover-up* technique?
8. By what procedure is a *suffix* that begins with a vowel added to a *root word* that ends in an *e*?
9. What is a *morpheme*?
10. Why must *polysyllabic words* be divided into syllables before they can be *sounded out*?
11. How are *contractions* formed?
12. What elements of structural analysis can be found at the preprimer level?
13. What is an *abbreviation*?
14. By what procedure is a *suffix* that begins with a vowel added to a *root word* that contains a single vowel followed by a single consonant?
15. Why are *nonsense words* sometimes used for *syllabication* practice?
16. How do *inflectional endings* differ from *derivational suffixes*?
17. What is a *compound word*?
18. When no other clues are present, where is the *accent* placed on most two-syllable words?
19. How is a *plural noun* ending in *s* changed to the *possessive form*?
20. In what way can the practice of *looking for little words in big words* cause later problems for students?

DEFINITION AND IMPORTANCE OF STRUCTURAL ANALYSIS

Structural analysis is the examination of words for meaningful parts. This skill is often used in conjunction with phonics. In fact, syllabication (one aspect of structural analysis) must be used before phonic analysis can be applied to *poly-syllabic* or *multi-syllabic* words

(words of more than one syllable). Phonic generalizations pertaining to vowel sounds are useful only with short words, words of one syllable, or with single syllables of longer words.

Prefixes and suffixes are termed *affixes*. They are attached, or affixed, to root words. Prefixes, suffixes, and root words are also referred to as *morphemes*. A morpheme is the smallest unit of language that conveys meaning. Many words are comprised of more than one morpheme as they contain more than one unit of meaning.

Knowledge of common prefixes, suffixes, and root words can enable students to recognize literally thousands of words that might otherwise be unknown to them. Affixes, (prefixes and suffixes) have a high degree of predictability. Prefixes consistently occur before root words, and suffixes occur after root words. Both prefixes and suffixes are usually spelled the same and pronounced the same in all the words in which they occur. Additionally, all prefixes form separate syllables as do most suffixes.

The reading problems of older students are often related to their inability to decode words of more than one syllable. They may have difficulty reading a word with a prefix or suffix even when they know the root word. Additionally, vowel sounds can cause problems for older students who did not thoroughly understand them when they were first taught phonics. As was noted earlier, syllabication must be used before the vowels can be sounded in longer words. Therefore, most older students can benefit from some work with structural analysis.

Generally, when adults meet unknown words they look for common syllables, syllables whose pronunciation and meaning are familiar to them. They mentally sound known prefixes, roots, and suffixes almost automatically. The readers of this book may have done this type of *sounding out* when they encounterd the word *polysyllabic* earlier in this section. Adult readers use structural analysis without consciously knowing they are doing so. However, individuals are not born with this ability. Children must be taught to use structural analysis.

Simple elements of structural analysis can be taught to students when they first begin to read; moreover, older students can benefit from a broad foundation of this important word recognition skill. Knowledge of structural analysis is a definite asset when a student encounters a word that is not in his sight vocabulary and he finds context clues inadequate. Structural analysis can enable the student to quickly pronounce and attach meaning to the word.

LEARNING STRUCTURAL ANALYSIS

As with phonics, teachers must be thoroughly familiar with all aspects of structural analysis if they are to successfully teach it to their students. Therefore, the content of structural analysis is presented in the subsequent sections. This content includes various elements of structural analysis as well as the related topics of syllabication and accent. Finally, various principles of structural analysis instruction are discussed.

Content of Structural Analysis[3]

This section outlines five basic elements of structural analysis. Syllabication and accent, both aspects of structural analysis, are also presented.

Elements of Structural Analysis

1. A *root word* or *base word*, as it is sometimes called, is a single word that may stand alone or may be combined with additional word parts. In the following examples, *friend* is the root word:

friend *friends* *unfriendly*

2. A *suffix* is an affix that is attached to the end of a root word. There are two primary types of suffixes. One type is referred to as *inflectional endings* and the other as *derivational suffixes*.

a. *Inflectional endings* are the most common suffixes attached to root words. Inflectional endings that affect number are: *s* and *es* *(girls, dresses)*. Endings that affect tense are: *s*, *ed*, and *ing (walks, walked, walking)*. Endings that affect degree are *er* and *est (taller, tallest)*. *Plurals* and *possessives* can both be formed by the addition of inflectional endings. They are further explained below.

(1) The *plural* form of a word indicates more than one.

[3]Based on Woodington, C.C. and Perry, L.A.: *Teaching the Reading Teachers* (Springfield: Thomas, 1983), pp. 59-61, 64.

Plurals are usually formed by the addition of an inflectional ending that affects number (*s* or *es*). Additionally, spelling patterns dictate the manner in which most plurals are formed.

(a) Most words can be made plural with the addition of the letter *s*. Examples are:

car, cars *stove, stoves* *chair, chairs*

(b) Words ending in *s, ss, sh, ch, x,* and *z* are usually made plural with the addition of the letters *es*.[4] Examples are:

bus, buses *dress, dresses* *brush, brushes*
church, churches *fox, foxes* *buzz, buzzes*

(c) Words that end in a *y* that is preceded by a consonant are made plural by changing by *y* to *i* and adding *es*. Examples are:

city, cities *baby, babies* *party, parties*

(d) Words that end in an *f* (or *f* plus final *e*) are made plural by changing the *f* to *v* and adding *es*. If a final silent *e* follows the *f*, the *e* is dropped before the suffix is added. Examples are:

calf, calves *knife, knives* *leaf, leaves*

(e) Some words are made plural by a spelling change rather than by the addition of an *s* or *es*. Examples of irregularly spelled plurals are:

goose, geese *child, children* *mouse, mice*

(f) For some words the plural and singular forms are the same. Examples are:

deer *moose* *sheep*

(2) The *possessive* form of a noun indicates ownership. Possessives are formed by the addition of an apostrophe and the letter *s* (*'s*) to the end of the noun. When the plural form of a noun ends in *s* the possessive is formed by the addition of an apostrophe after the *s*. Additionally, if the singular form of a noun ends in *s*, an apostrophe is added after the *s* to show

[4]The author tells her students that words ending in a *hissing* sound need an *es* to make them plural.

ownership.[5] Examples of the possessive forms of nouns are:

Singular noun: *Tyson's jacket*

Plural noun ending in *s*: *the girls' hats*

Singular noun ending in *s*: *Chris' raincoat*

b. *Derivational suffixes* are attached to the end of a root word and usually affect the meaning of that word. Examples of derivational suffixes are:

able (comfortable) *ful (colorful)*
less (odorless)

c. The spelling of a root word is sometimes affected by the addition of a suffix:

(1) If a root word ends in a *y* that is preceded by a consonant, the *y* is changed to *i* before most suffixes are addeed. However, if the suffix begins with the letter *i*, the *y* is not changed. Examples are:

hurry, hurried *pretty, prettiest*
fly, flying

(2) If a root word ends in the letter *e* and the suffix begins with a vowel, the final *e* in the root word is dropped when the suffix is added. Examples are:

ride, rider *glide, glided* *rake, raking*

(3) If a root word contains a single vowel and ends with a single consonant, the final consonant is doubled before adding a suffix that begins with a vowel. Examples are;

run, running *stop, stopped* *wet, wettest*

3. A *prefix* is an affix that is attached to the beginning of a root word. Prefixes affect a word's meaning. Examples of prefixes are:

dis (disconnect) *pre (preview)* *un (unhappy)*

4. A *compound word* contains two distinct root words. The pronunciation of both root words is retained and usually a meaning derived from both is reflected in the new word's meaning.[6] Examples of compound words are:

grandmother *football* *birthday*

5. A *contraction* is the shortened form of two combined words. An

---

[5]A few teaching aids suggest that all nouns be made possessive by the addition of *'s* regardless of their spelling *(Chris's book)*.

[6]Words such as *forget* and *carpet* are not compound words.

apostrophe is placed where the letter or letters are deleted. A contraction retains the original meaning of the two words but takes on a new pronunciation.[7] Additionally, some contractions have irregular spellings. Examples of contractions are:

they have, they've   *did not, didn't*   *will not, won't*

Syllabication and Accent

Syllabication and accenting skills are both needed by students when they attempt to pronounce unknown words of more than one syllable. Principles for both are discussed below.

SYLLABICATION. When a student encounters an unknown word of more than one syllable, he must possess the necessary skills to enable him to divide the word into syllables before he can apply phonic analysis. The manner in which a written word is divided into syllables is not always the way the word is pronounced. However, the division of most words is close enough to enable a student to arrive at an approximate pronunciation. Additionally, when a student divides a word into syllables, he must make certain that each syllable contains a vowel sound. Syllabication principles are:

1. When two consonants occur after a vowel, divide the word between the consonants (*bub/ble, win/dow*).
2. When a single consonant occurs after a vowel, divide the word after the vowel (*pu/pil, na/tion*).
3. In a word that ends in *le* preceded by a consonant, the consonnt plus the *le* make up the final syllable (*la/dle, rat/tle*).
4. Generally, medial consonant blends and digraphs are not divided in a word. The whole blend or digraph is usually sounded in the same syllable (*fast/er, kitch/en*).
5. Most suffixes constitute separate syllables (*quick/ly, un/tie*).
6. Compound words are divided between the two words that comprise them (*fire/man, rain/coat*).

ACCENT. In words of two or more syllables, one syllable will usually receive more stress when the word is spoken. A student can place the accent on a selected syllable, and if this choice does not result in a word that *makes sense*, he can place the accent on another

[7] Contractions are often more accurate representations of speech than the whole words they represent.

syllable. Additionally, a student needs to have some knowledge of accenting in order to effectively use the dictionary as an aid to pronunciation.

In two-syllable words, the first syllable is usually accented when there are no other available clues. Principles of accenting are:

1. In a word containing double consonants, the first syllable is usually accented (*let' ter*).
2. When the second syllable has a consonant plus *le*, the first syllable is usually accented (*pud' dle*).
3. A first syllable ending in *ck* will usually be accented (*nick' el*).
4. Words ending in *y* usually have accented first syllables (*han' dy*).
5. Compound words usually have an accent on or within the first word (*cow' boy*).
6. Words containing three or more syllables often have both a primary and a secondary accent (*es' ca la' tor*).
7. In words with prefixes or suffixes, the primary accent will usually fall on or within the root word (*re fresh' ing*).
8. Words with two vowels in the second syllable will usually have an accented final syllable (*con vince'*).

Principles of Structural Analysis Instruction

Students can begin to learn some of the basic elements of structural analysis as they first learn to read. Plural nouns, such as *pigs* and *hats*, are usually found in the first preprimer of a basal reader series. Possessive forms of nouns (*Tim's dog*) and compound words (*birthday*) can also be found in the earlier levels of a reading series. Additionally, contractions (*I'll*) are sometimes included at these levels. The inclusion of these elements in beginning readers is evidence of the need for structural analysis instruction to insure that young readers can effectively deal with these word forms.

Since suffixes are easier to learn, young children should be taught common suffixes prior to being taught prefixes. When a suffix has been added to a word, the root word comes first. Thus, children can use clues from the root word to help them decode the word's inflected or derived form. Teachers should always use familiar root words (those already in the students' sight vocabularies) when teaching new suffixes.

In addition to plural and possessive endings, beginning readers are taught the *ed* and *ing* endings. Inflectional endings are easier for students to learn; therefore, they should be taught before derivational suffixes. After students have learned some of the more common suffixes, they are then introduced to prefixes. No precise order exists for instruction in the elements of structural analysis. However, teacher's manuals that accompany basal readers provide a recommended sequence for teaching these various elements. Teachers who use an approach other than a basal reader series should consult additional sources for a recommended sequence.

Just as students are taught to recognize root words by sight, they can also be taught to recognize affixes by sight. If students can instantly recognize a large number of affixes, they are better equipped for independent reading. Students also need to be taught that the letters that comprise a prefix may not be a prefix in all words. For example, the letters *un* form a prefix in the word *untie* but not in the word *uncle*.

Earlier, structural analysis was defined as the examination of words for meaningful parts. This description should not be confused with looking for little words in big words. Looking for words in other words can lead to problems when children attempt to pronounce the entire word. For example, if children pronounce the word *fat* in the word *father* before they attempt to pronounce *father*, the result will be confusing to them.

Syllabication can sometimes be difficult for students to master. In order to effectively use syllabication, students should be taught that after they divide a word into syllables, they should sound out the syllables as if they were separate words. Moreover, students should sound the vowels and the consonants according to the phonic generalizations they have learned.

When providing practice with syllabication, a teacher should begin by using words the students already know. After the students have mastered a particular syllabication principle, they should practice dividing unknown words into syllables. If a teacher requires students to divide only words they already know, she cannot be certain if they have mastered the skill or if they are dividing the words by the way they know to pronounce them. Furthermore, older students can also practice syllabication skills on nonsense words.

Abbreviations are sometimes considered a part of structural analysis. Students need to be made aware that abbreviations are a shortened form of a longer word or phrase and that they are usually followed by a period. Students also need to know that abbreviations are pronounced the way the original word or phrase is pronounced.

When teaching structural analysis, teachers should not have students memorize various elements as *rules*. Instead, students should be guided to form their own generalizations. For example, if a teacher wished to teach students to drop a final *e* before adding a suffix that begins with a vowel, she could write the words *hide* and *hiding* on the board. She could then let the students tell what happened to the *e*.

As with phonic analysis, overemphasis on structural analysis should be avoided. Many times context clues are adequate and a student has no need to use structural analysis or phonics. Teachers should always keep in mind that students read for pleasure and to obtain information, not so that they can decode words.

APPLICATION OF STRUCTURAL ANALYSIS

Complete the following exercises on structural analysis.

1. Give four examples of *morphemes*.
2. What is the *plural form* of these nonsense words?

a. ren	b. wos	c. pech
d. tady	e. fash	f. bloss
g. druf	h. neep	i. bix

3. Change these phrases to the *possessive form*.
   a. the suitcase that belongs to Connie
   b. the bicycles that belong to the girls
   c. the soccer ball that belongs to Roger
   d. the horses that belong to Kris
4. Indicate the manner in which an *ed* would be added to these nonsense words.

a. lape	b. bly	c. mibe
d. frop	e. yun	f. screg

5. Which of these words contain *affixes*?

a. preview	b. roundtable	c. blest
d. disconnect	e. unit	f. untie
g. readable	h. distance	i. tallest

6. Which of these words are *compound words*?

a. raincoat	b. cowboy	c. carpet
d. fireman	e. forget	f. doghouse

7. Divide the following nonsense words into *syllables*.

a. faddle	b. iptob	c. haber
d. wistner	e. tabben	f. rackly

8. Identify the syllable on which the *accent* would fall in these nonsense words.

a. pellow	b. zuddle	c. tofblain

CLASSROOM APPLICATIONS

Most basal reader series provide for the development of all word recognition skills, including structural analysis. However, there are many things a teacher can do to expand upon what is taught in the basal. The author has found the *cover up* technique particularly useful for helping students analyze unknown words containing affixes. When she listens to one of her students read orally and the student encounters an unknown word with an affix, the author covers up the affix or says something like, "Cover up the *ed*." Usually, the student can pronounce the root word. He then reattaches the affix and pronounces the entire word.

Similar directions can be given to a student who encounters an unknown word when he is reading silently and asks the teacher for help with the word. If the unknown word contains both a prefix and a suffix, the student should be told to first remove the prefix and then remove the suffix before decoding the root word. Finally, he reattaches the suffix (or suffixes), then reattaches the prefix and pronounces the word in its entirety.

After a student has pronounced a word he has decoded, his oral language ability will help him determine if the word makes sense in the passage in which it occurred. Derived and inflected forms of words are already a part of students' speaking vocabularies, thus enabling them to more readily recognize these word forms.

A student's oral language will also help him determine the sound given certain suffixes such as *ed*. The *ed* ending can sound like *t, d, ed,* or *id*. In some words the *ed* forms a separate syllable (*wanted*) and in some words it does not (*jumped*). Variations of this nature usually do not cause problems for students. Therefore, teachers need not be overly concerned about teaching all the different pronunciations.

Any time a teacher can actively involve students in the learning process, the students are more likely to remember what they are being taught. Activity-oriented lessons are particularly beneficial for young students, who often have short attention spans. An activity might be helpful if a teacher wanted to teach the meanings of the *er* and *est* endings. She could place three of the students side by side to illustrate *tall, taller*, and *tallest*.

A teacher could also use students to demonstrate the formation of compound words. Various words could be written on cards and passed out to the students. The teacher could call out a particular compound word. The students who had the words that comprise that compound word could go to the front of the room and place their word cards together. A similar activity could be done with contractions.

Syllabication skills, usually stressed in the upper elementary grades, can be introduced to young students through a variety of approaches. Oral exercises should precede written exercises. Oral exercises can help students hear the number of syllables in a word. Students can tap or clap the beats of the syllables. Some teachers have their students put their hands under their chins. They tell them to say a particular word and feel how many times their chins go down. The number of times their chins go down indicates the number of syllables in the word.[8]

For structural analysis, as for other word recognition skills, incidental learning often occurs. For example, when the author was having her students read a story that she had written for them for St. Patrick's Day, several students were puzzled by the abbreviation *St.* The author saw the opportunity to talk to the students about abbreviations. She explained that *St.* was an abbreviation for the word

[8]This procedure is effective because a person's chin goes down when he makes a vowel sound. Each syllable contains a vowel sound; therefore, the chin drops on each syllable.

Saint. She further explained several other abbreviations *(Mr., Dr., ft.)*. To avoid later confusion, she told them that *St.* was also used as an abbreviation for the word *Street*. Teachers will often find that opportunities for incidental learning, such as the one just described, can be used to create student interest in numerous structural analysis concepts.

STRUCTURAL ANALYSIS POSTTEST

1. Define *structural analysis*.
2. Why must a student divide a word into syllables before applying phonic analysis?
3. What are *affixes*?
4. Define *morpheme*.
5. Why would it be unwise to delay structural analysis instruction until students have been in school for several years?
6. Define *base word*.
7. Compare and contrast *inflectional endings* and *derivational suffixes*.
8. In what way do spelling patterns affect the formation of *plurals*?
9. How can a *plural noun* ending in *s* be changed to show ownership?
10. What change is made to a *root word* that ends in an *e* before adding a *suffix* that begins with a vowel?
11. Describe the change made to a *root word* containing a single vowel followed by a single consonant before a *suffix* that begins with a vowel can be added.
12. Define *compound word*.
13. Describe the formation of a *contraction*.
14. Where is the *accent* placed on most two-syllable words?
15. Identify four elements of structural analysis that are often found in preprimers.
16. Is it easier for children to learn *prefixes* or *suffixes*? Why?
17. How can *looking for little words in big words* result in confusion for students?
18. Defend the practice of using *nonsense words* for reinforcement of *syllabication skills*.
19. Define *abbreviation*.
20. Outline the *cover-up* technique as it was described in this chapter.

DICTIONARY USAGE

In this final portion of Chapter 4, dictionary usage will be discussed. Dictionary usage is taught in conjunction with the other word recognition skills: sight words, phonics, context usage, and structural analysis.

The *dictionary usage pretest* in the following section can be used by the reader to assess his/her knowledge of dictionary usage.

DICTIONARY USAGE PRETEST

1. Do students *master* words when they look them up in the dictionary and write their definitions?
2. In what way can a teacher serve as a *role model* in the area of dictionary usage?
3. What are the *locational strategies* that should be taught to students?
4. What three courses of action might a student be likely to take when he meets a word he cannot decode and context clues are lacking? What course of action would be more desirable? Why?
5. How can *picture dictionaries* be useful for introducing young children to dictionary usage?
6. What are the *pronunciation strategies* that should be taught to students?
7. When is *dictionary usage* considered a word recognition skill?
8. What is a prerequisite for learning *alphabetical order*?
9. What features should be considered when selecting a dictionary for student use?
10. How can telephone books and mail-order catalogs be used for practice with alphabetical order?
11. What *meaning strategies* should be taught to students?
12. What is *etymology* and how can it be used to interest students in using a dictionary?

DEFINITION AND IMPORTANCE OF DICTIONARY USAGE

Dictionary usage is considered to be both a word recognition skill and a study skill. When regarded as a word recognition skill, it refers to the use of a dictionary to derive the correct pronunciation and meaning of an unknown word.

Dictionary usage is more valuable for students above the primary grades than it is for younger students. Upon encountering a word not in his sight vocabulary, a student may unsuccessfully attempt to use context, phonics, or structural analysis. Furthermore, he may arrive at a pronunciation of the word through the use of phonics and/or structural analysis but still not know the word's meaning. When an older student decodes a word that is not in his listening or speaking vocabulary, he must know how to effectively use a dictionary. Dictionary usage enables a student to become a truly independent reader.

LEARNING DICTIONARY USAGE

As with context usage, the discussion of dictionary usage does not contain any lists of generalizations.[9] Instead, the types of strategies needed by students for effective use of the dictionary are presented. Additionally, several principles of dictionary usage instruction are suggested.

Dictionary Strategies[10]

The dictionary skills needed by students fall into three categories: locational strategies, pronunciation strategies, and meaning strategies.

Locational Strategies

To arrive at the correct pronunciation and meaning of an unknown word, a student must first be able to locate the word in a dictionary. The following locational strategies are needed by students:

1. A student must know the sequence of the letters of the alphabet (alphabetical order) and understand how the order is used in a

---

[9]For this, the reader should be grateful.

[10]Based on Woodington, C.C. and Perry, L.A.: *Teaching the Reading Teachers* (Springfield: Thomas, 1983), p. 70.

dictionary.

2. He must be able to use the guide words found at the top of the pages of a dictionary.
3. He must possess adequate structural analysis skills, as the unknown word (in context) may be a derived or inflected form of the entry word in the dictionary.

Pronunciation Strategies

After a student has located an unknown word in the dictionary, he must be able to pronounce the word. These pronunciation strategies should be taught to students:

1. A student must be able to use the pronunciation key at the beginning of a dictionary and its shortened version at the bottom of various pages.
2. He needs to know how syllables are indicated in dictionaries and understand the use of primary and secondary accent markings.
3. He must also understand the use of phonetic respellings and diacritical markings.

Meaning Strategies

Finally, a student must be able to use a dictionary to determine the meaning of an unknown word. These meaning strategies are needed by students:

1. A student must learn how to select the most appropriate meaning for the context in which the unknown word appeared.
2. Additionally, the word in the selected passage may be a derived or inflected form of the entry word found in the dictionary. Therefore, a student must learn to adapt a dictionary's meaning to the context of the passage.

Principles of Dictionary Usage Instruction

While adults often consult a dictionary when they encounter unfamiliar words, children are frequently reluctant to do so. If their decoding skills (and context clues) are inadequate, they are usually not sufficiently motivated to *look up* a word in a dictionary. A student may simply skip over the word or say another word in its place. If an adult is nearby, the student may ask the adult to tell him the word.

However, skipping an unfamiliar word or saying another word in its place interferes with a student's comprehension of the passage. Additionally, older students should not have to be dependent on adults to help them with words. Therefore, dictionary usage is a skill that definitely needs to be developed if students are to become independent readers.

Knowledge of alphabetical order is one of the skills a student must possess before he can locate a word in a dictionary. Obviously, a student must first know the names of the letters of the alphabet before he can utilize alphabetical order.

A teacher will occasionally find students above grade one who have not mastered all the letters. This lack of letter knowledge is more prevalent with students who have reading disabilities. A child who can say the letters in order is not necessarily able to recognize each letter. Therefore, a teacher who wishes to assess a child's letter knowledge should present the letters to the child in random order.

In the early grades, groundwork for later dictionary usage can be laid. Developmental instruction in the use of alphabetical order can be started in grades one and two. For young children, instruction in alphabetical order can be enhanced through the use of picture dictionaries. While not all of these dictionaries have entries arranged in alphabetical order (some are arranged by categories), they can give children an enjoyable *first experience* with dictionary usage.

Students do need to be taught how to use a dictionary's pronunciation key in order to quickly and successfully pronounce a previously unknown word. However, a teacher would not want to require students to memorize the pronunciation key used in a particular dictionary, as these keys may differ from one dictionary to another.

Teachers should keep in mind that students do not necessarily master a word by looking it up in a dictionary and writing its definition. Instead, students must be made aware that many words have multiple meanings. To obtain the correct meaning for an unknown word, they should read all the word's various meanings and refer back to the context in which the word appeared. This technique will enable them to select the most appropriate meaning. Moreover, dictionary work should include oral discussion to clear up any misconceptions students might have.

Finally, caution should be exercised when a teacher is selecting a dictionary for student use. A number of excellent dictionaries are available and teachers should *shop around* when looking for an appropriate one. These features should be a consideration when selecting a dictionary: (1) the size of the dictionary and its number of included entries should not overwhelm the students, (2) the format should clearly distinguish each entry, (3) definitions should be written at an appropriate reading level, and (4) for each given meaning of a word, a sentence should be provided that illustrates that meaning.

APPLICATION OF DICTIONARY USAGE

Complete the following exercises on dictionary usage.

1. Which would be the best format for assessing a student's letter recognition?
   a. a b c d e f g h ...
   b. f s p b t m a x ...
2. Indicate which type of *dictionary strategy (locational, pronunciation,* or *meaning)* is needed in the following situation.
   Tim has located a word in the dictionary but is uncertain of the vowel sounds in the word.
3. Which type of *dictionary strategy* is needed in this situation?
   Leslie needs to know on which page of the dictionary she should look for a word she has encountered in her reading.
4. Identify the type of *dictionary strategy* needed by this student.
   The word that Connie has located in the dictionary has several meanings and she needs to know which one fits the context of the passage she was reading.
5. Which type of *dictionary strategy* does this student need to use?
   Ty is uncertain about whether the word *carport* comes before or after the word *carpet*.
6. Place the following words in *alphabetical order*.

a. mountain	b. partner	c. napkin
d. party	e. octopus	f. parsley
g. particular	h. radio	i. mother

7. Indicate which of these words would be located on a page whose

guide words are *janitor* and *javelin*.

a. jaundice b. jargon c. jangle
d. jaw e. jar f. January

8. Select the most appropriate meaning for the word *examination* as it is used in the sentence, "Cindy made a good grade on her examination."
   a. the act or process of examining
   b. an exercise to test knowledge
   c. an informal interrogation

CLASSROOM APPLICATIONS

As was mentioned earlier, a student must know how to use alphabetical order to enable him to locate a word in a dictionary. Skill in the use of alphabetical order can be developed in a variety of ways. The author has successfully used telephone books and mail-order catalogs for practice with this skill. These readily available materials teach the skill in a practical and enjoyable manner. Both sources lend themselves to an infinite number of activities that reinforce the use of alphabetical order.

Use of alphabetical order should also be emphasized with older students. Students in the intermediate grades should be able to alphabetize a list of words to the fourth letter. For review, they can complete exercises that require them to supply the letter that precedes or follows a given letter. They could also be asked to determine in which third of the alphabet a particular letter occurs. However, whenever possible, activities and exercises should be ones that allow students to see a purpose for learning the use of alphabetical order or other related dictionary skills.

Excellent commercial materials are available that teach dictionary usage. When selecting a source to teach dictionary skills, a teacher should look for one that stresses the aspects of dictionary usage that she plans to teach.

Etymology—the study of word origins—can be an exciting way to interest students in using the dictionary to learn more about words and their meanings. Older students can be challenged to discover the derivations of words that are of interest to them. An unabridged dictionary can be obtained from the school library and used for such word study. Once students have gained sufficient skill in the use of the dictionary, they are more likely to consult it on their own when they encounter unknown words in their reading.

Finally, a teacher who shows an interest in using a dictionary can be a good model for her students. If she frequently consults a dictionary in the presence of her students, they will realize that dictionary usage can be a valuable skill to acquire. Enthusiasm is contagious!

DICTIONARY USAGE POSTTEST

1. In what way is *dictionary usage* considered a word recognition skill?
2. Describe the *locational strategies* needed by students for effective dictionary use.
3. What *pronunciation strategies* should students acquire?
4. Describe the *meaning strategies* needed by students.
5. Relate what most students do when they encounter an unknown word that they cannot decode (and context clues are inadequate). Describe a more desirable alternative.
6. What must a student first know before he can be taught *alphabetical order*?
7. How might a teacher use a *picture dictionary* to introduce dictionary usage to young children?
8. Defend or condemn the practice of having students look words up in the dictionary and write their meanings.
9. What should a teacher look for before purchasing a dictionary for classroom use?
10. Outline a procedure for using telephone books and mail-order catalogs for practice with alphabetical order.
11. Define *etymology*. How might a teacher use etymology to motivate students to use the dictionary?
12. How can a teacher's enthusiasm for consulting a dictionary influence student attitude toward dictionary use?

CHAPTER 5

COMPREHENSION SKILLS

IN the previous three chapters, the reader became acquainted with the five word recognition skills. Word recognition skills enable students to recognize words they encounter in their reading.

Chapter 5 focuses on comprehension skills, the skills that enable students to derive meaning from what they read. Comprehension skills are taught concurrently with word recognition skills.

Prior to reading this chapter, the reader should take the *comprehension skills pretest* to assess his/her knowledge of comprehension skills and comprehension instruction.

COMPREHENSION SKILLS PRETEST

1. What is the primary purpose of reading?
2. What are the four *levels of comprehension*?

3. Why is reading without comprehension not really reading?
4. When is the best time to begin comprehension instruction?
5. At which level is a student comprehending when he recalls explicitly stated information?
6. What are purpose-setting questions?
7. How is a student's *experiential background* related to his ability to comprehend written materials?
8. Which level of comprehension involves *reading between the lines*?
9. How can young students be helped to distinguish fantasy from reality?
10. What is meant by *recalling sequence*?
11. Why might some students comprehend only at the *literal level*?
12. For what reason should students acquire the ability to detect propaganda?
13. At which level of comprehension might an emotional response to a written selection occur?
14. What is the primary method used to develop comprehension skills in students?
15. How is comprehension related to memory?
16. What are some of the causes of comprehension problems?
17. Why is the ability to follow written directions important?
18. How should a teacher handle incorrect responses to comprehension questions?
19. Why does a student need to learn to mentally summarize what he reads?
20. What advantage do most students have when they encounter figurative language in written passages?

DEFINITION AND IMPORTANCE OF COMPREHENSION SKILLS

Comprehension is basically a thinking activity. It is deriving meaning from what is read. A student who *reads* without comprehending is not really reading.

When a student comprehends, he reads a passage and assigns meaning to that passage. He then relates what he reads to his previous knowledge. This combination of previous knowledge and new information allows him to both understand the author's message develop new concepts and ideas. Occasionally, the student will make immediate use of the new information in some manner.

Regardless of whether or not the student puts the new information to use, these newly acquired concepts become part of his background knowledge for further reading and learning. Thus, reading comprehension is part of a continuous process whereby the student adjusts what was previously read and learned and combines those concepts with newly read information.

The first step in comprehension is the understanding of word meaning. The reader must understand the meaning of the words used by the author. He is then able to see the relationships between these words and the phrases, sentences, and paragraphs of the written passage. He is able to see how these elements relate to each other, how they contribute to the passage as a whole, and how they are used to communicate the author's message.

A student must be able to do more than just *read the words*. Fluent oral reading does not necessarily indicate comprehension. A student may be able to read aloud beautifully but not know anything about what he has read. Teachers need to keep in mind that the ability to pronounce a word does not mean that the student understands the word's meaning.

Comprehension involves memory. A student must be able to recall what he reads. Comprehension also involves reflective thinking as the student draws on past experiences and relates what he reads to those past experiences. Students should *picture in their minds* what they are reading about. These mental pictures are then available for later recall as the student needs the information.

The primary purpose of reading is to obtain meaning. Therefore, if students do not develop adequate comprehension skills, reading will not be beneficial to them. If a student lacks the ability to comprehend written passages, then it will not matter how proficient he is in word recognition skills. The lack of comprehension skills will prevent him from being able to obtain meaning from what he reads. Word recognition skills serve only to make comprehension possible; good readers have the ability to recognize words *and* understand the author's meaning.

Comprehension skills, while important in all reading situations, become crucial when students engage in content area reading. If students have not learned how to comprehend stories in their basal readers, they will have even greater problems in the upper elementary grades and in junior and senior high school, where they are required to read a variety of types of written materials. A student who is unable to understand what he reads in his science, social studies, and math textbooks will have difficulty in all of these subjects. (See Chapter 6 for a thorough discussion of reading in the content areas.)

From the above discussion, one can conclude that comprehension skills are very important and must be developed if students are to obtain meaning from what they read. The following sections will enable teachers to better understand the nature of these comprehension skills and how they can be developed in students.

LEARNING COMPREHENSION SKILLS

Comprehension skills do not encompass a clear-cut, specific set of skills as do some of the word recognition skills. There exists, however, several distinct levels of comprehension to be developed in students. The following sections provide an overview of these levels of comprehension. This overview is followed by a discussion of various principles of comprehension instruction.

Levels of Comprehension

The four levels of comprehension are: literal, inferential, critical, and creative. Prior to the discussion of each of these levels of comprehension is a listing of the levels along with their characteristic skills. This listing will help the reader visualize how the levels of comprehension are interrelated.

Levels of Comprehension Skills[1]

1. *Literal Comprehension*
   Recognizing and/or recalling of:
   - Details
   - Main ideas
   - Sequence

---

[1]Woodington, C.C. and Perry, L.A.: *Teaching the Reading Teachers* (Springfield: Thomas, 1983), p. 66.

    Comparison
    Contrast
    Cause and effect
    Directions
    Character traits
2. *Inferential Comprehension*
  Inferring:
    Details
    Main ideas
    Sequence
    Comparison
    Contrast
    Cause and effect
    Directions
    Character traits
  Summarizing
  Generalizing
  Drawing conclusions
  Predicting outcomes
  Interpreting figurative language
3. *Critical Comprehension*
  Separating fact from opinion
  Distinguishing fantasy from reality
  Determining relevancy and adequacy
  Judging accuracy
  Detecting propaganda
  Identifying author's purposes, biases, and authority
4. *Creative Comprehension*
  Responding emotionally
  Using information in a new situation

Literal Comprehension

As was noted in the previous section, literal comprehension is the recognition or recall of literally stated facts, details, etc. This means that the student who is comprehending at the literal level recognizes and/or recalls information that was explicitly stated in the written passage. However, the level of difficulty at which the passage was written influences a student's ability to extract literally stated information. For example, the details contained in one passage may *stand out* much more than they do in another passage. Consider the following:

> Connie went to the store to buy a dress. She got a pretty blue one. When she got home she put the dress on. She looked very pretty in her new dress.
>
> Question: What color was Connie's new dress?
>
> Jill needed a new dress for the party. She went to the department store and tried on a blue dress. She wasn't sure that she liked the dress, so she went to the dress shop next door. There she tried on a pretty green dress, but that dress was too short. Then Jill went to a new store across town and saw a pretty pink dress. But that dress cost too much. So Jill went back to the department store and bought the dress she had tried on there.
>
> Question: What color was Jill's new dress?

The color of the girls' new dresses is a detail of little importance, except maybe to their dates who might be planning to purchase corsages to match the dresses. The passage illustrates, however, that literally stated information in some selections may be easier to recall than that in other selections.

Literal comprehension is considered the lowest level of comprehension. However, contrary to what many persons would have teachers believe, *lowest* does not mean that literal comprehension is in any way inferior to the other levels of comprehension. It simply means that students usually must be able to comprehend written materials at the literal level before they can comprehend at other levels.

For many students, literal comprehension may be the highest level at which they can comprehend. For some remedial reading and special education students, even literal comprehension is quite an accomplishment.

Students who are just learning to read may comprehend primarily at the literal level. While there is nothing wrong with encouraging young students to comprehend at *higher levels*, there is also no cause for alarm if their comprehension is mainly at the literal level.

In order to provide the reader with a better understanding of what is involved in literal comprehension, the eight aspects of literal comprehension listed earlier will be defined and discussed.

DETAILS. The student examines the passage for literally stated details. Details are those facts or ideas that usually answer the questions *who?, what?, when?, where?,* or *which?*

Obviously, not all details are importnt. Questions carefully formulated by the teacher prior to a reading assignment can help students focus on the *key* details. A student who tries to remember all the minute details of a story may be overwhelmed by the task.

Teacher guidance is necessary for each reading assignment, as details that are important in one context may not be important in another. As illustrated in the following passage, some details support the *main idea* while others do not.

> Ty and Jay were playing ball. Their ball got stuck in a tree. The boys got a wooden ladder and got the ball out of the tree. Then they started playing ball again.

"What kind of ladder did the boys use?" "Why did the boys use the ladder?" One of these questions points to a detail that is important to the passage while the other does not.

MAIN IDEA. The main idea of a passage is its central theme. It is the *main message* that the author is conveying to the reader. While the main idea is included in literal comprehension, often it is not explicitly stated but is inferred. When the student has to infer the main idea of a passage, the skill is considered a part of inferential comprehension.

In a longer selection, a student can often note the topic sentences of various paragraphs and determine the main idea of the passage from those sentences. Additionally, titles of written selections often suggest the main idea. This author insists that her students always read titles and subtitles to find out what the story is going to be about.

As was noted above, some details serve as support for the main idea. It is through the use of these supportive details that an author communicates his message to the reader.

What is the main idea of this passage?

> Cindy planted rose bushes. She worked hard to care for the bushes, and every year the bushes were covered with pretty yellow roses. One year she did not have time to take care of the roses. She hoped her husband, Jimmy, would take care of them, but he did not have time either. The rose bushes died because

no one took care of them.

SEQUENCE. The sequence of a passage is the order in which the various events take place. In an earlier passge, Jill went to several different stores before she purchased a dress for the party. The passage told where she went first, second, third, and last (which was also where she went first). In that passage, the sequence of events was described.

Note the sequence of events in this pasage:

> Mrs. Coleman was helping clean her daughter's house. First they moved the table and chairs off the kitchen floor. Then they scrubbed the floor.
>
> While they were waiting for the kitchen floor to dry, they dusted the living room furniture and cleaned the living room carpet.
>
> By then the kitchen floor was dry so they moved the furniture back onto the floor. They looked at the kitchen clock and it was almost lunchtime. After all that work, they decided that they should go out for lunch.

An understanding of the sequence of the passage helps a student recall the events described and see how those events were related to each other. While sequence is more important to some selections than others, having students recall the order of events is a very beneficial aid to comprehension.

COMPREHENSION AND CONTRAST. When a student looks for comparisons in a selection, he looks for ways in which one person, object, place, or concept is similar to another. When he looks for contrasts, he looks for differences between persons, objects, places, or concepts. An understanding of the comparisons and contrasts drawn by an author will contribute to the student's understanding of the passage as a whole.

Consider the comparisons and contrasts in the following:

> Ann and Julie are sisters. Ann is a college student and Julie is a high school student. They both like the same kind of music and both like to dance. Ann has brown hair and Julie is blond. Julie lives in Arizona and Ann lives in Missouri.

CAUSE AND EFFECT. To discover cause and effect, the student looks for information in a passage that indicates that a particular occurrence was caused by something else. As with other areas of literal comprehension, determining cause and effect is easier for some passages than others. The following passage illustrates an obvious cause and effect:

> Every year the Perrys had a beautiful lawn. It was thick and green and almost free of weeds. Last spring it got very warm and the grass started to come up, just like it does every year. But then it got very cold again. Frost covered the ground every morning for a number of days. Later, when warm weather came to stay, the grass did not grow. The weeds grew, but there was no grass. The cold weather had killed the grass.

DIRECTIONS. The ability to follow written directions is a skill needed by students both in and out of school. The successful completion of many school assignments is dependent upon the student's ability to accurately read and follow the directions that were given.

In many out-of-school situations students will find the need to follow written directions. Whether they construct a small computer or give a friend a permanent, accurately following written directions is usually required.

Note the directions given in this passage:

> To make popcorn, place ¼ cup vegetable oil in the base of the popcorn popper. Then add ⅔ cup popcorn to the oil. Place the cover of the popper on the base and plug the unit into an outlet.
>
> When the popping cycle is complete, unplug the cord. Then invert the entire unit so that all the popped corn is in the cover. Season and serve.

CHARACTER TRAITS. In order to better acquaint their readers with the characters of a story, authors mention various traits of those characters. In this manner they *develop* the characters. Recognizing character traits helps a student understand why the character acts in a particular manner. The student should be able to extract enough information about a character so that he feels he *knows* him as well as he would a real person.

What character traits are indicated in this passage?

> Mrs. Bryant expected her fourth-grade students to work hard. She gave them extra work to challenge them. If they did not understand how to do something, she took the time to explain it to them. She truly cared about her students and they

knew it.

Inferential Comprehension

Inferential comprehension is more difficult for a student than literal comprehension, for it requires that the student supply meanings that were not directly stated in the written passage. When engaging in inferential comprehension, the student uses explicitly stated facts and ideas to infer other facts or ideas that were not directly stated in the passage.

Inferential comprehension is often referred to as *reading between the lines*. This ability to attach additional meaning to literally stated information depends in part on the student's background. The information a student already possesses influences the amount and type of information he will be able to extract from a written passage.

Often a rereading of a particular passage will uncover elements that went unnoticed on the first reading. A careful rereading is sometimes required if the student wishes to look further into the passage in order to infer information that was not stated outright.

As was previously mentioned, inferential comprehension may be beyond the reach of students of limited ability and of students who are just learning to read. However, all students should be given the opportunity to *try out* inferential comprehension on appropriate written materials. Experienced teachers are the best judges of how much to expect from their students in the area of inferential comprehension.

As with literal comprehension, the various elements of inferential comprehension will be discussed individually to enhance the reader's understanding of this level.

INFERRING DETAILS, ETC. The eight aspects of literal comprehension may be inferred if they are not literally stated. The student can infer details, main ideas, sequence, comparison, contrast, cause and effect, directions, and character traits.

Obviously, a single written passage is not likely to contain all eight of these aspects, whether they are literally stated or must be inferred. The student must be guided to determine what types of information can be inferred from the selection he has read.

SUMMARIZING. After a student reads a written passage, he needs to be able to mentally summarize the information contained in the passage. This ability to summarize helps the student later recall what he has read.

Summarize the facts presented in this passage:

> Central Methodist College is a private, four-year liberal arts college. Approximately 700 young men and women attend the coeducational institution. Central Methodist is located in Fayette, Missouri, midway between St. Louis and Kansas City. For over 130 years Central Methodist has provided students with a quality education in a caring atmosphere.

GENERALIZING. When a student generalizes he forms a basic principle, or generalization, based on the information provided in the written selection. Caution must be exercised in this area, for it is possible that the student can get *off track* and form an invalid generalization. Additionally, the information provided by the author is sometimes insufficient for the student to use in forming a generalization.

The following passage does contain sufficient information for a generalization to be formed. From the passage, one can generalize that a positive self-concept contributes to school success.

> Mrs. Tuttle's students were having trouble with their reading. They didn't feel very good about themselves or about reading. However, she praised them each time they did well and encouraged them to keep working hard and keep learning new words.
>
> Mrs. Tuttle gave her students stickers when they did particularly well. Getting stickers made them feel really good because they knew it meant their teacher thought they were reading well. Soon the students had learned many new words and were ready to start reading a more difficult book.

DRAWING CONCLUSIONS. Based on the information provided in the passage the student determines what is really going on, what the *main drift* of the passage is. He draws a conclusion from statements or facts provided by the author.

What conclusion can be drawn from the following?

> The big day will soon arrive. In preparation for the event, James and Virginia have been shopping for needed items. They went to the department store and bought two baby beds. They

also bought a double stroller and two high chairs. "How many diapers to you think we'll need?" asked Virginia.

PREDICTING OUTCOMES. When a student predicts outcomes, he anticipates what will happen next in a story or other written selection. Predicting what will happen next helps the student comprehend a selection even if the outcome is later revealed.

Young children who are just learning to read can be guided to predict outcomes. The illustrations used in most materials for beginning readers often aid young students in anticipating what will happen next. In materials written for older students, outcomes are sometimes more difficult to predict.

The outcome of the following can be easily predicted:

> Leslie was floating on an air mattress at the swimming pool. She was trying hard not to get her hair wet because she had a meeting to go to that night. Just then, Ty did a *cannonball jump* off the diving board right next to where Leslie was floating.

INTERPRETING FIGURATIVE LANGUAGE. The student needs to be made aware that not all written statements are to be taken literally. Many times, written passages will contain expressions whose meanings are different from what is indicated on the surface.

Students can transfer to their reading the knowledge they have of figurative language used in speech. Most students would know that "It was raining cats and dogs" does not mean that it was literally raining small domestic animals. Likewise, "He was making a mountain out of a molehill" is not likely to be taken literally by students who have heard the expression used in speech.

The following passage contains examples of figurative language:

> Tim and Tommy had had problems with the computer before, but it really had them over a barrel this time. Tim said, "You know this computer program has to be running by tomorrow morning." "You're pulling my leg," said Tommy. "No I'm not," said Tim. "I got it straight from the horse's mouth. If it's not running we're going to be up the creek."
>
> Just then the solution came to them. You could have knocked them both over with a feather! "We've got the tiger by the tail," said Tommy. "Yeah. It's in the bag," said Tim.

Critical Comprehension

After students are able to comprehend on the literal and inferential levels, they are then guided to develop critical reading. While reading critically is usually taught in the upper elementary grades, some elements of critical comprehension can be taught as early as grade one. For example, students learn to distinguish fantasy from reality when they determine that the animal character in a story cannot really talk.

Critical comprehension requires that the student evaluate what he reads. This evaluation involves analytical thinking. While engaging in critical comprehension, the student is mentally questioning all aspects of the written selection.

As with other levels of comprehension, teacher guidance is needed if the student is to develop the ability to read critically. Critical comprehension is developed over a period of time through the use of carefully selected materials.

To further clarify what is involved in critical comprehension, examples of critical reading skills will be discussed individually.

SEPARATING FACT FROM OPINION. Students who are accustomed to believing everything they read often are surprised to learn that not everything in print is factual. They need to realize that sometimes what they are reading may represent the author's opinion rather than actual facts. Through critical evaluation of a written passage a student should be able to determine whether the passage is based on fact or opinion.

Does this passage represent fact or opinion?

> In hot weather no one feels like going outside. It is just too hot to do much of anything. But in cold weather people can put on their coats and go sledding, ice skating, snow skiing, and lots of other neat things. Cold weather is much nicer than hot weather.

DISTINGUISHING FANTASY FROM REALITY. It would seem that even young children could easily distinguish fantasy from reality: something is either real or it isn't. However, some things that used to be considered fantasy, such as space travel, are now reality. Also, through the use of special effects, fantasy on television and in the movies often appears to be real. Therefore, some children may have difficulty distinguishing between fantasy and reality in their reading.

To aid students in distinguishing between these two forms of writing, teachers can have the students ask themselves the question, *"Could this really happen?"* The following passage illustrates an event that could not really happen and is, therefore, fantasy:

> Linda and Joyce both had just built new houses. Their yards were very bare. They wanted shrubs and flowers in front of their houses, but they both knew that planting shrubs and flowers is a lot of work. So Linda got out her magic stick and waved it around each place that she wanted something planted. Soon her house was surrounded with beautiful shrubs and flowers. Then they went to Joyce's house to make her yard beautiful too.

DETERMINING RELEVANCY AND ADEQUACY. As the student examines a particular source, he needs to be able to determine if the information it contains relates to the topic about which he seeks information. He also must be able to determine if the information is adequate for his purposes. If the selection contains information that is not relevant to the topic or is an inadequate treatment of the topic, the student will need to seek alternative sources.

Is the passage below a relevant and adequate discussion of the characteristics of the sun?

> The sun gives off heat and light. The moon, on the other hand, has no heat or light of its own. The moon's surface is cool. People have even walked on the surface of the moon. Rocks that astronauts found on the moon are on display at museums in the United States.

JUDGING ACCURACY. When judging accuracy, the student must decide if the written passage is free from error. Based on prior knowledge, he determines if the information given is accurate or correct. If prior knowledge is lacking, the student can be guided to consult additional sources in order to verify the accuracy of the source in question.

Is the information in the following passage accurate?

> In the years following the Great Depression, the United States began making preparations for World War I. The factories that produced war-related materials provided employment for those who lost their jobs during the Depression.

DETECTING PROPAGANDA. Through mass media advertising students are constantly bombarded by propaganda. This constant exposure necessitates that they acquire the ability to detect propaganda in all forms, including written materials. A student who is accustomed to believing everything he reads may have difficulty recognizing written statements designed to persuade him to think or act in a particular manner.

Propaganda is evident in this passage:

> If these two school districts merged, everything would be so much better. A great deal of money could be saved and there would be a definite improvement in the quality of instruction. A "yes" vote on Proposition 39 will provide better educational opportunities for your children.

IDENTIFYING AUTHOR'S PURPOSES, BIASES, AND AUTHORITY. As the student critically reads a selection, he should ask himself why the author wrote the selection. He should also try to identify any biases the author might have that are evident in the writing. Additionally, the student should try to determine if the author's background indicates that he is likely to have knowledge of the topic about which the selection was written.

Is the author of this passage likely to be knowledgeable about his topic?

> As a medical doctor with twenty-five years experience, I can conclusively say that most reading problems are caused by the lack of phonics in the schools. If the teachers would teach more phonics, there would not be as many children with reading problems.

Creative Comprehension

Creative comprehension is the fourth and final level of comprehension. However, it is not the most difficult type of comprehension for students to develop. Certain aspects of creative comprehension are considerably easier for students than some aspects of inferential or critical comprehension. For example, even a very young student can respond to a question like, *"What would you do if you found a $10 bill like Kyle did in the story?"*

To aid the reader in understanding what is involved in creative comprehension, the elements of this level are discussed below.

RESPONDING EMOTIONALLY. When responding emotionally to a selection, the student reacts to it in a personal manner. He *interacts* with the selection, then *reacts* to it in some way. He may react to what he read by indicating a like or a dislike for the selection. As the student develops his reading tastes, he will no doubt have preferences for certain types of writing.

The student might also make a value judgment regarding the actions of one of the characters. This value judgment may be the result of his *putting himself in the character's place*. What type of value judgment is a student likely to make regarding the actions of the character in the following passage?

> Todd was driving his mother's car. He skidded on the ice and hit a parked car. No one was looking so he quickly drove off, hoping that no one saw him.

USING INFORMATION IN A NEW SITUATION. Sometimes when a student reads a particular selection, he is able to make immediate use of the information contained in that selection. Perhaps the student had been having a difficult time controlling the ball when he played soccer. If he locates a helpful book on soccer techniques, he may be able to achieve better ball control by making use of the information provided by the author.

Likewise, information contained in written selections can sometimes be applied to situations other than those for which it was designed. A student who reads a book on painting techniques may be able to transfer what he learns about painting to the use of other media such as felt-tipped markers and colored chalk.

A girl who is always late to school because she rarely hears her alarm go off can easily relate to Gloria's situation in the passage below. She may then make use of the information in the passage to solve her own problem.

> Gloria was late to school three days last week. The principal said that if she was late again, she would have to go to in-school suspension.
>
> Gloria had to think of something to help her hear her alarm clock. Suddenly, she got an idea. She got a metal pie pan from her mother's kitchen. She put her clock inside the pan so that the alarm would echo off the metal when it went off. "This should

wake me up," she said.

Principles of Comprehension Instruction

Comprehension instruction should be started when students first begin to read. Comprehension skills should be taught concurrently with word recognition skills so that the primary instructional emphasis is on *understanding* what is read.

A basal reader series will introduce and develop various comprehension skills throughout the entire series. As comprehension is developed mainly through teacher questioning, questions are usually provided in the teacher's manual for use with each reading selection. Additionally, comprehension questions are found in the workbooks and sets of duplicating masters that accompany basal readers.

Comprehension is highly related to a student's oral language and experiential background. The ideas and concepts that a student already possesses are often as important to comprehension as those he obtains from the actual reading. Prior to having students read a selection, the teacher can ask questions to assess their background knowledge of the topic about which they will read. She can then *fill in the gaps* so that they will have a sufficient background to enable them to adequately comprehend the selection. Providing this conceptual framework is particularly important if the students are reading in the content areas where background knowledge may be lacking.

To aid comprehension, teachers can also ask purpose-setting questions prior to having the students read a selection in their basal readers. These questions serve to guide the students' reading of the selection. They should be carefully formulated and should be applicable to the particular selection that the students are about to read. The teacher can encourage *higher level* thinking by asking thought-provoking questions. She should include questions that require the students to comprehend on the inferential and critical levels if the ability of the students and the type of reading material in use are adequate for these levels of comprehension.

Following the reading of a selection, follow-up questions are asked. Follow-up questions should reflect the purpose that was set during the discussion prior to the reading. If a student reads to find answers to questions that the teacher asked before the reading, and the teacher asks entirely different questions after the reading, the student will conclude that he must read very slowly and *take in* everything. This will result in the student being unable to focus on the important aspects of the selection. When follow-up questions do not reflect the purpose-setting questions, they are not effective for guiding and evaluating comprehension.

When helping a student comprehend a written selection, the teacher can guide him to see how he can use what he already knows and combine it with what he is reading to obtain the answer to the questions she has asked. Teachers should make certain that they allow adequate time for their students to respond to questions. Often, students barely have enough time to give a quick answer before the next question is asked. Students will be encouraged to *think out* their responses if they know they will be given enough time to do so.

Comprehension is enhanced when the teacher guides the student in obtaining a correct answer rather than simply telling him that his oral or written response was incorrect. If the student does not learn why his answer was incorrect, he may continue to make inappropriate responses in the future. Also, incorrect responses should always be handled tactfully. A student should not be made to feel uncomfortable when he makes an incorrect response. An atmosphere of acceptance in the classroom enhances all learning, including reading comprehension.

The teacher needs to constantly assess a student's responses in order to determine how the student can be helped to comprehend successfully. If, after reading a selection silently, a student cannot answer questions over what he has read, the teacher can ask him to read a short passage orally. If he miscalls a number of words, the material is too difficult for him. He will need to be placed in easier material and given additional instruction in word recognition skills, particularly sight words.

Other comprehension problems may be caused by noisy surroundings or other factors that cause a student to be easily distracted. If the student is tired, hungry, or sick, he is likely to have difficulty comprehending what he reads.

If a written passage contains difficult language patterns, the student may have problems understanding the author's message. Also, as was noted earlier, a lack of sufficient background for a particular selection can result in comprehension difficulties.

Finally, a student may have difficulty comprehending because he reads at an inappropriate rate. He may read so fast that he overlooks important concepts or so slowly that the meaning is lost. Excessively slow reading may be due to a limited sight vocabulary. The student may simply not know a sufficient number of words to enable him to read and comprehend the selection.

As students sometimes have difficulty transferring to the actual reading process what they learn in isolated drill, comprehension practice should be accomplished using actual reading materials as much as possible. Additionally, the more a student reads, the better he will develop comprehension skills. Through wide reading a student will be exposed to a variety of written materials and writing styles and will develop techniques for comprehending these diverse materials.

Comprehension is enhanced when a student reads about a topic in which he is interested. He is likely to get more out of something he *wants* to read than something imposed on him by others. To build comprehension skills, a student should read many books at his independent level, the level at which he can read without teacher assistance.

Finally, students do not have to be questioned over everything they read. They should be permitted to read some things simply for enjoyment without being quizzed about what they have read.

APPLICATION OF COMPREHENSION SKILLS

By completing these exercises the reader can apply some of the concepts presented in Chapter 5.

1. Infer the main idea of this passage:

   At first, Lisa did not like her new school. She did not know anyone and she was afraid that she would not make friends. However, she soon made many new friends and was glad she had gone to that school.
2. Write a short paragraph containing three examples of figurative language.
3. At what level is this student comprehending?

After Joy read the book about the Civil War, she concluded that it was not very objective. She said that she detected a strong anti-Northern sentiment in the author's account of the war.

4. Predict the outcome of the situation described in this passage:

   The elementary education student went to her reading class most of the time. But she never read her textbook or took notes in class. When it came time for a test, she borrowed her roommate's notes. Later, when she got her first teaching job, she realized that she knew very little about teaching children to read.

5. What level of comprehension is indicated in this example?

   Jean got out the manual that came with her new personal computer. By following it carefully, she was able to design and run the program that she needed.

6. Write a paragraph containing propaganda.
7. What conclusion can be drawn from the information contained in this passage?

   Mrs.Kent went back to college to finish her degree. She had difficulty finding time to do her school work because she was so busy keeping up with the activities of her three daughters. However, in spite of all the demands on her time, she was able to complete her degree and start her new job. Then she found that all her experience in dealing with children really came in handy.

8. What level of comprehension did this student employ?

   Rob read a story about a boy whose dog had died. He told his teacher that he understood how the boy felt because his dog, Bif, was getting old and may die soon.

CLASSROOM APPLICATIONS

A readiness for reading comprehension can be developed even before students begin to read. Through picture reading, students can develop skills such as finding details, determining the main idea, noting cause and effect, and predicting outcomes.

Listening comprehension can also be developed at the prereading level. The teacher can read a selection to the students and utilize both purpose-setting and follow-up questions. Listening comprehension activities help build memory skills that are needed for reading comprehension.

After students enter the beginning reader stage, careful preparation for each reading task will enhance comprehension. The discussion that takes place before the students begin a reading assignment is the time that the teacher assesses the students' background for the topic. She then provides them with additional information if she finds their background for the topic is limited.

This author has a very extensive picture file that she uses to provide background information (and to generate interest in a topic). Pictures were chosen that relate to various selections in the basal reader series. The pictures were placed in file folders and arranged in the order that they appear in various levels of the basal. Before her students read a selection on frogs and tadpoles, for example, the author shows them some pictures of frogs and tadpoles. Viewing the pictures promotes discussion and prepares the students for the selection they are about to read.

As was stated earlier, purpose-setting questions are asked by the teacher before the students read a particular selection. These questions can serve to introduce the selection, arouse interest, and motivate the students to want to read the selection.

In addition to assessing background knowledge, extending conceptual framework, and setting the purpose for reading, the teacher should introduce key words that the students will encounter in the reading selection. If the teacher introduces key words to the students before they begin the reading, comprehension problems caused by unfamiliar words (or the unfamiliar use of known words) can sometimes be prevented.

After the students have finished reading a selection, the follow-up questions asked by the teacher can be used to evaluate the students' comprehension. These questions can also serve to summarize what was learned. If pictures that pertain to the selection were shown prior to the reading, they can be viewed again following the reading.

Many excellent commercial materials are available to help students develop comprehension skills. These materials usually contain short written passages followed by comprehension questions. Materials are available at all reading levels and cover a wide range of comprehension skills.

In addition to using commercially available materials and a basal reader series, teachers can provide their students with comprehension practice in a variety of ways. For example, sequencing skills can be taught on several different levels. Young students can sequence the pictures from a comic strip that has been cut apart. After students have read a story, they can sequence sentences from the story that have been written on strips of paper. They could also dictate the story to their teacher in their own words. This author has found this dictation technique very effective for developing sequencing and other aspects of comprehension.

Following written directions can be practiced in a variety of settings. The teacher can even develop this skill during an art lesson. All the directions for engaging in the activity could be written rather than spoken.

Many activities can be used to help students infer the main idea of a written selection. The teacher can clip newspaper articles and separate the articles from their titles. Students can read the articles and match them with the title that best illustrates the main idea. Newspaper articles can also be used to help students learn to summarize. After reading several articles, the students can write brief summaries of the information presented in the articles.

To help students develop the ability to predict outcomes, the teacher can read the first half of a short story and then ask the students to predict the outcome. The teacher could then read the rest of the story to let the students see if they were correct.

Asking the questions "How did you know?" or "Why do you think . . .?" can help students determine if their inferences are correct. The author frequently has her students locate the sentence or sentences that contained the clues they used in determining their answer.

To develop critical reading skills, a teacher can use oral exercises to prepare students for written activities. For example, one team of students could issue a statement and let another team decide if the statement represented fact or opinion. The students could also analyze items on the editorial page of a newspaper. They could then compare these items with items that appear on the front page of the same newspaper to see if the editorial page is based on fact or opinion.

In helping students learn to detect propaganda, the teacher can have them look for *loaded words* in advertising. Various television advertisements can be analyzed in addition to ads appearing in newspapers and magazines. Students can be guided to determine which portions of the advertisements are fact and which are opinion.

Creative comprehension, like the other levels of comprehension, can be developed in a number of ways. The teacher can have the students create an alternate ending for a story they have just read. She can ask them what they think and/or feel about what they have read by using questions such as: "What would you have done if you were in the same situation that the character in the story was in?"; "Has anything like this ever happened to you?"; "How did you feel?"; "What did you do?"

The above-mentioned activities are a few examples of the many types of things teachers can do to effectively develop comprehension skills in their students. Additional ideas for developing all levels of comprehension can be found in numerous resources available to teachers.

COMPREHENSION SKILLS POSTTEST

1. When should comprehension instruction be started?
2. Elaborate on the primary technique used for developing comprehension skills.
3. Identify the four levels of comprehension.
4. Describe an effective procedure for using purpose-setting questions.
5. Of what importance is the ability to follow written directions?
6. *Reading between the lines* characterizes which level of comprehension?
7. Describe an appropriate technique for handling incorrect responses to comprehension questions.
8. Summarize why some students might comprehend only at the *literal level.*
9. In what way can young students be helped to distinguish fantasy from reality?
10. An emotional response to a written selection is characteristic of which level of comprehension?
11. In what way is memory involved in comprehension?
12. Describe the relationship between a student's *experiential background* and his ability to comprehend written materials.

13. Explain what is meant by *recalling sequence*.
14. Review some of the possible causes of comprehension difficulties.
15. In what way is summarizing a useful tool?
16. Explain the primary purpose of reading.
17. Identify the level of comprehension that involves the recognition and/or recall of explicitly stated information.
18. Speculate on why students whose primary language is English have an easier time interpreting figurative language than do students for whom English is a second language.
19. Explain why fluent oral reading without comprehension is not really reading.
20. Elaborate on the importance of teaching students to detect propaganda.

BE
TOPS
KEYS
TO
GOOD
SPELLING
UP
TO

CHAPTER 6

READING/STUDY SKILLS

THIS chapter emphasizes the use of reading/study skills which are most frequently associated with instruction in the content areas. These skills are used by students as they *read to learn*.

The goal of this chapter is to insure that the reader recognizes and masters the components of each reading/study skill presented and becomes aware of the use of these skills in content areas and/or reading classroom(s). The *reading/study skills pretest* below will enable the reader to assess his/her knowledge of reading/study skills and their instructional value.

READING/STUDY SKILLS PRETEST

1. What are *reading/study skills*?
2. What is *content-area instruction*?
3. Why is every content-area teacher a reading teacher?
4. Why should content-area teachers *not* assume students know how to use reading/study skills in the content areas?
5. What are the five major reading/study skills for most content areas?
6. What skills must a student master to *locate* a reading source and a specific passage within the source?
7. How does a student use *alphabetizing* in locating a passage to be read?
8. What information can be found on the title page of a book?
9. How can a student find a book in the *card catalog* in the library?
10. What skill is used when *locating* a topic in most reference sources?
11. Describe four types of *dictionaries*.
12. What does an *encyclopedia* offer a student?
13. What is an *atlas*?
14. How does a student most quickly find a needed article in a *periodical*?
15. What are three situations in which a reader uses *selection* skills?
16. What are the four main *organizational patterns* used in content-area writings? What is a *signal* word for each of these four devices?
17. If the reader cannot recognize the organizational pattern on which a writing is based, what should the reader immediately locate to determine the contents of the passage?
18. Why should a student *take notes*?
19. What process should a content-area teacher use to teach *outlining*?
20. Compare and contrast *summarizing* and *synthesizing*.
21. Describe how a student would *flexibly* read a passage.

22. What is a *graphic aid*? List three examples of graphic aids.
23. What is the purpose of a *circle graph*?
24. Why must a student know what is contained in the *legend* of a map?
25. Distinguish between lines of *latitude* and *longitude*.
26. How should a teacher require the student to correlate a map with his reading assignment?
27. How does the teacher incorporate the *teach, practice, apply* process to the teaching of reading/study skills in the content areas?
28. What is *readability*? How is it determined?
29. What factors does a teacher consider in the selection of a textbook for content-area use?
30. How does a reading/study strategy improve a student's content-area reading? Give an example of one such strategy and its steps.
31. How should a teacher construct a test for a unit of study in a content area?

DEFINITION AND IMPORTANCE OF READING/STUDY SKILLS

Whereas the skills presented in Chapters 2 through 4 are those necessary for the student to *learn to read*, reading/study skills enable a student to *read to learn*. Reading/study skills are applied by the student so that he can more ably comprehend, interpret, organize, and apply pertinent reading materials to study needs. Use of these skills enable the student to spend less time with an assignment and yet comprehend more.

As earlier shown, the teaching of reading at the elementary level emphasizes the mastery of skills over a period of years. Most reading instruction centers around a basal reader series. The stories are written with an emphasis on teaching the student how to read with little or no consistent training in the use of reading/study skills. Therefore, as the student progresses into the upper elementary grades, teacher guidance is essential to enable the student to learn to use reading/study skills in various school subjects.

In most school situations, emphasis is placed on content-area instruction at the beginning of the fourth grade. *Content-area instruction* is the individual teaching of a specific subject area (e.g. science, mathematics, English, social studies). The primary focus is on the students' understanding and continual use of the concepts of a subject area. These *concepts* are the ideas that develop the central or main theme of a unit of study.

Engrained within this instruction are principles of reading. Often, teachers assume that students who can read can easily master content-area reading materials. As a result, little effort is placed on showing the students how to read these materials. Consequently, some students do not perform at a satisfactory level. The incorporation of reading/study skills instruction in a content area can often raise the students' level of performance and simultaneously ease teaching demands as the students can more readily understand their assignments.

The reading/study skills needed for each content area varies. However, for study in each area, the student must know how to select appropriate materials and how to use the selected sources to obtain necessary information. Secondly, he must be able to organize information gained in order to retain, utilize, and transfer it to other learning situations. Thirdly, the student should develop a flexible reading rate so that the reading material is under his control. Finally, the student should develop an awareness of graphic aids (e.g. pictures, graphs) that enhance comprehension. The student's use of these aids increases comprehension and later serves as a mechanism for reviewing the material covered.

The use of each of these elements of reading/study skills should be developed in accordance with the students' reading demands and the teacher's instructional techniques. To avoid reading failure and negative attitudes toward the content-area subject, the content-area teacher must: (1) correctly place the students in appropriate reading materials; (2) teach the reading skills necessary for success in the content area; and (3) demand constant application of these skills through classroom instruction.

LEARNING READING/STUDY SKILLS

As indicated, teachers frequently assume students have mastered reading/study skills necessary for successful performance in content-area subjects. They assume that an introduction to these skills in a basal reading program automatically enables students to transfer these learned skills to other areas of study. However, guidance in the use of the reading/study skills is necessary if students are to perform at the highest level possible. Thus, the foundation for these skills must be developed in the lower grades so that when the students later enter content-area studies their use of these skills is automatic.

For teachers to adequately develop an understanding and use of content-area concepts, they must grasp the correlation between reading/study skills and the mastery of content-area subjects. The two are intertwined. The teacher either takes advantage of her awareness of these skills and teaches them as *tools of the trade* or ignores them and allows the students to flounder through the content-area course. The following sections contain a discussion of each of the major categories of content-area skills.

Categories of Reading/Study Skills

Reading/study skills are categorized into five major areas. The areas include (1) location, (2) selection, (3) organization, (4) flexible reading rates, and (5) use of graphic aids. The following sections present each of these skill areas with their related subskills.[1]

Location of Reading Sources

Location of content-area information can involve the student in a variety of ways. Some learning situations totally rely on a single textbook as the reading source. Others include the use of reference materials located within the classroom; whereas, still others incorporate the use of the library and its materials. The skills necessary for success in these three situations are these: (1) ability to alphabetize, (2) ability to use book parts, (3) ability to function within the library, and (4) ability to utilize several types of reference sources.[2] This section examines each of these subskills from a practical viewpoint. It includes only the aspects of these skills that the student

[1]Based on Woodington, C.C. and Perry, L.A.: *Teaching the Reading Teachers* (Springfield: Thomas, 1983), pp. 25-28.

[2]The elements of these subskills are based on the items discussed under location skills in Cooper, J. David et al., *The What and How of Reading Instruction* (Columbus: Merrill, 1979), pp. 145-161.

needs in order to adequately function in a content-area classroom.

ALPHABETIZING. Although many types of material arrangements exist, the most commonly used is alphabetical order. Flexibility with this skill allows the student to use the index of a book, locate topics or key terms in general reference materials (e.g. encyclopedias and dictionaries), and locate articles in periodicals.

The student must locate information within an alphabetically arranged source as well as find a source that is arranged alphabetically among other reading materials on the library shelf. To do so, he must automatically and efficiently use the skill of alphabetizing. Use of this skill demands that the student: (1) know the alphabet and be able to correctly position each letter, (2) be able to arrange words by their first, second, and third letters, and (3) alphabetically arrange names and titles when locating a reading source by author or title.[3]

ABILITY TO USE BOOK PARTS. Whether a classroom is based on the use of a single textbook or includes the use of supplementary materials, a student must know how to use a book's parts. Instruction and consistent use of these various parts will enable the student to: (1) quickly determine if the book is appropriate for his needs, (2) readily locate information within the book, (3) better comprehend the information found, and (4) review ideas acquired.

The parts of a book that are the most help to the student in group and independent reading assignments include the title page, copyright page, table of contents, body of the book, and index.[4]

The *title page* provides bibliographic information about the book. Located on this page are the complete title, author's name, publishing company and its location, as well as other information concerning the book.

On the reverse side of the title page is the *copyright page*. The *copyright date*, located on this page, indicates how current the material is. Also located here are the rights of the publisher as to

[3]In the alphabetical arrangement of names, the last name is presented first, followed by the first and middle names. When arranging titles that begin with the words *a, an,* or *the,* these words are omitted, with the second word (or first major word) in the title being used to determine the title's proper placement.

[4]Additional book parts that are useful in detailed reading assignments are the preface, appendix, bibliography, and footnotes.

publication and reproduction of the material, information about the author(s) and illustrator(s), and Library of Congress classification information.

The sequence of chapters and subsections in a reading source are outlined in the *table of contents* by chapter number and beginning page. The table of contents allows the reader to determine the major topics found in the source as well as helps the student review the material. He can easily glance over the section titles of a chapter to see if he can clearly remember the key concepts presented in each section.

The organization of the *body of the book* is the format the author uses to present the content of the book. This organization includes the breakdown of the book into chapters, the subdivision of information within each chapter and the inclusion of graphic aids throughout the book. The student's purpose for reading may easily dictate the source he chooses. If he needs to have a general overview or outline of a topic, he should seek a source that breaks the chapters into subsections with summaries of each major section. Whereas, the student who selects a source to read for pleasure would prefer to read a selection characterized by continuous, uninterrupted reading within each chapter.

The *index* is of utmost importance in the use of a textbook and supplementary classroom materials. This book part alphabetically lists each topic in the book and indicates the pages on which the topic is discussed. Effective use of an index can eliminate much wasted reading time. By first consulting the index, the student can determine if a topic is discussed in the book and how many pages are devoted to it. Depending on the depth of his research, the student can decide whether the source is necessary or if it can be deleted from his reading selections. Otherwise, the student may read an entire selection, only to find that his topic is not adequately discussed.

ABILITY TO FUNCTION WITHIN THE LIBRARY. To adequately function within a library, the student must know and understand its organization. Essentially, this organization evolves around the card catalog and the location of the materials within the library itself.

To determine where materials are located in the library, the *card catalog* is used. This catalog locates materials by author, title, and subject.[5] Usually, this information is filed on cards in the card catalog; however, more and more libraries are beginning to file this information on microfiche or microfilm.

The number by which a reading source is filed within a library is the *call number*. It is found in the left corner of each catalog card. This number is matched to that number found on the spine of the book or other designated location or nonbook materials. Without this number, the book cannot be easily located.[6]

Ability to Use General Types of Reference Materials. The student who is expected to use supplementary learning materials will often first consult general reference sources. The format and purpose of each of these materials dictate the necessary location skills to be used. However, most require the use of the card catalog to locate the source, alphabetizing to locate the topic within the source, and organization of the information. Typically, the reference sources used at the elementary and/or secondary level include the dictionary, encyclopedia, atlas, and periodicals.

A *dictionary*, as a reference source, provides a student with an alphabetical listing of words. It enables him to locate a word for pronunciation, definition, and use in speech. The words and information embodied within a dictionary depend on the type of dictionary used.

As a student progresses through the grades, he will be exposed to various types of dictionaries. At the early stages of reading development, *picture dictionaries* are appropriate. These dictionaries include an illustration with each entry word. Words portrayed in such dictionaries are those that are concrete in nature and that automat-

[5]The first line of the *author card* provides the reader with the author's last name followed by his first name. The title is first shown on the *title card*, and appropriate subjects make up the first line of the *subject cards*. Each of these three cards is filed alphabetically by its top line. Information on each card also includes the call number, author's name, title, publisher, copyright date, and paging information. Subject information is listed on the title and subject cards only.

[6]Commonly, the call number belongs to one of two library classification systems: the Dewey decimal classification system or Library of Congress system. The Dewey decimal system is based on ten numerical classifications and is primarily used by smaller libraries. The Library of Congress system, on the other hand, has twenty such categories with each consisting of a letter followed by numbers. The advantage of this latter system is that it provides more classification combinations and enables publishing companies to catalog materials when they are printed. The preassignment of this classification number results in greater consistency throughout the various library systems.

ically bring a picture to the reader's mind.

During the elementary years, the *elementary dictionary* is found in most classrooms. These dictionaries include those words that an elementary student would be likely to encounter. The entries are written at an easy reading level. The print is larger than in most dictionaries, and illustrations accompany some of the individual entries.

The *unabridged dictionary* is complete, as it includes all words in the English language and contains a more comprehensive entry for each word. The *abridged dictionary* deletes lesser-used words found in the unabridged dictionary. Both are commonly used above the elementary level. *Specialized dictionaries* are also available for specific areas (e.g. music). Each concentrates on those terms essential to a particular area.

For the student to use any dictionary, basic skills are required. The complexity of the skills depends on the nature and level of dictionary. (Chapter 4 elaborates on the skills commonly used with the dictionary.)

The *encyclopedia*, a single- or multi-volumed source, alphabetically embodies a general discussion of topics. Like dictionaries, some encyclopedias are written on an easy reading level for younger students, while other volumes are designed for more sophisticated study. The number of topics included and the depth of discussion is determined by the audience for which the source is designed. Furthermore, the encyclopedia can be general in nature or can be developed around a specific area of study. The skills needed to adequately use the encyclopedia as a reference source encompass all of the reading/study skills analyzed in this chapter.

An *atlas*, another general reference source, is a collection of maps. As with the encyclopedia, an atlas can be comprehensive, general, or specialized in its coverage. Most frequently, a general atlas is used to locate maps of various regions or countries of the world. A more specialized atlas is limited to maps of a particular type (e.g. physical or political) or to a limited area (e.g. the fifty states of the United States).

The purpose and scope of an atlas dictates the subject portrayed in the maps. It also determines the often accompanying statistical data that details, enlarges, or explains the information portrayed through the maps. To effectively use an atlas, the student must be able to: (1) locate a map within its contents, (2) determine by the key or legend if that map is relevant to his research needs, and (3) fit his findings into his learning assignment. (See later section that discusses map skills.)

As a student's research skills become more advanced and he is expected to utilize more supplementary reading sources, the student will incorporate into his research a greater variety of general reference tools. One such reference tool is a *periodical*. Periodicals include sources that are available on a regular, reoccurring basis (i.e. magazines, journals, newspapers, almanacs, yearbooks, and directories). Most frequently, these periodicals are published on a monthly or weekly basis. The reader must be proficient in the use of reading/study skills if he is to effectively use periodicals to supplement general reference sources such as an encyclopedia or textbook.[7]

Regardless of the collection of reference sources available to the reader, few will be consulted if instruction and repeated practice of necessary reading/study skills does not occur. The ease and confidence with which the student uses a source and adapts the newly found information into the format of his assignment will largely determine the usefulness of the source to him. A student should not be expected to utilize information available only in a reference source that is too difficult for him to read. Reading/study skills are useless if the words are incomprehensible.

Of primary importance is the purpose for using a reference source. If the reader is not aware of how a reference source will be an aid to his reading purpose, learning will not result. A reference source is helpful only if the student can adequately utilize it to obtain needed information.

Selection of Reading Sources

After locating potential informational sources, the student must select the source that most adequately meets his needs. He then determines the specific passage that supports his reading purpose. Se-

---

[7]If the student has access to a large number of periodicals and uses these regularly, he should be taught how to utilize the *Reader's Guide to Periodical Literature*. This guide alphabetically lists periodical articles by subject, author, and title and indicates their location in specific periodicals. Use of this index simplifies the reader's research by eliminating the need to scan through the individual issues of the periodicals to locate an article on a particular topic.

lection skills are used when the student has access to only one source and must select the passage pertinent to his reading needs; when he must isolate from several sources the one that will best meet his needs; or when he must combine the essential aspects of several sources to obtain a complete, balanced overview of the topic.

In selecting a reading source, the student will rely heavily on organizational skills and on the format of the source to determine its relevancy. He first focuses on headings, key words, and phrases, and summary paragraphs that are highlighted in the source. Beyond this initial glance at the reading passage, the student will rely on the organizational pattern around which the author has presented his ideas. (See the section on organizational skills for a discussion of organizational patterns.)

The student's rate of reading greatly determines the effectiveness of his selection skills. By skimming the reading passage in search of organizational elements, he should be able to rapidly estimate the usefulness of the material and not waste valuable time. (See the section on "Flexibility in Reading Rates.")

Selection skills are necessary for the organization and culmination of a reading assignment. When the student can automatically use selection skills, he will quickly and accurately eliminate unnecessary, unprofitable informational sources, and thus focus on sources that directly relate to and aid his reading purpose.

Organization of Information

Location and selection of a reading source are preliminary steps to the student's organization of information into a final product. This phase of reading/study skills should occupy a major portion of the time the student spends on his assignment. To organize information, the student flexibly reads to determine the writer's main points and organizational patterns as they pertain to his purpose. He then puts this newly learned information into his own words. Organization skills require the student to: (1) recognize organizational patterns of reading sources, (2) take notes, (3) outline, (4) summarize, and (5) synthesize.

Recognition of Organizational Patterns. Before the student can respond to a written passage, he must first read and comprehend the passage. If the student is flexible in his reading, he will comprehend more information at a faster pace. (See the section on

"Flexibility in Reading Rates.") Yet, a flexible rate of reading can only be effective if he recognizes the writing's organizational patterns.

An *organizational pattern* is the format selected by the writer to express his ideas throughout a reading passage. Most writers utilize one of several of these frameworks to structure their ideas in a more orderly and understandable manner in a single passage as well as throughout an entire book. These patterns include *main idea, chronological order, comparison/contrast*, and *listing*.[8] As the student reads, it is to his advantage to recognize the *signals* of these organizational patterns. In skimming the material, the organizational device should become readily apparent. The student then can adjust his reading rate to focus on the pattern as it relates to his reading purpose.

For those passages that are not structured in an obvious organizational pattern, the reader should immediately seek to find the *main idea(s)* and *supporting details* of the writing. The main idea expresses the central theme of a writing, while supporting details contain information contributing to these main thoughts. (Chapter 5 thoroughly discussed these comprehension skills.)

The reader should develop the habit of first skimming a reading passage for the main thoughts as reflected through headings, summary paragraphs, and/or the first sentence of each paragraph. If none of these techniques help to determine the central theme, then the individual paragraphs should be skimmed in search of the main ideas and their supporting details.

Ideas organized by *chronological (time) order* are presented sequentially. The passage is organized to reflect the order in which events occurred or their sequence of importance. Words that signal chronological order to the reader include *before, after*, or specific dates. *Initially* and *subsequently* are also indicative of chronological order, in that they indicate passage of time or the occurrence of significant, related events.

When *comparing* two ideas, the writer is illustrating how the two are alike. He uses such words as *because, thus, as well as*, and *similarly*. When contrasting ideas, the differences between the two are stressed through key words such as *either . . . or, on the other hand*, and *yet*.

---

[8]Based on Herber, H.L.: *Teaching Reading in Content Areas*, 2d ed. (Englewood Cliffs: Prentice-Hall, 1978), pp. 72-102.

When the writer seeks to present several ideas that are of equal weight and are discussed in no sequential order, a simple *listing* is utilized. Included can be a discussion or the mere identification of each listed item. Numbers, as well as words that indicate numbers such as *first, second,* and *lastly*, signal a listing in a written passage.

NOTETAKING. To outline, summarize, or synthesize information gathered from a reading source, a student must first take notes.[9] Notetaking is essential if the student is to later recall ideas from a reading (or listening) experience. This skill prevents a student from forgetting what he read or heard when later recall is required.

Notetaking is only useful to the student if he is allowed to *personalize* his writing into a style with which he is comfortable. The technique he selects must be the one he can use automatically and effectively later when recalling what was previously read.

In taking notes, the *content* is more important than the format. A student's notes must have meaning for him and not necessarily for anyone else. Thus, instruction in the skill of notetaking differs from instruction for many other skills. These concepts should be instilled in students:

1. Notes should be brief with enough information to be comprehensible after a period of time.
2. The notes should be in the student's own words and not words taken directly from the reading source. Direct quotations should be included only when an author's statement is essential to the assignment or the student's reading purpose. When using direct quotations, the student should be careful to copy the quotation exactly and to indicate that it is a direct quotation. This care will prevent later confusion between quotations and notes taken in his own words.
3. The notes should consist mainly of key words, phrases, or short sentences that indicate the main idea and major supporting ideas of the selection.
4. The student should be introduced to several methods of notetaking: outlining; key words, sentences and phrases; and summary paragraphs. Practice should be followed by experimentation so

[9]Concepts for the skills of notetaking, outlining, and summarizing are based on Roe, B.D. et al.: *Reading Instruction in the Secondary School* (Chicago: Rand McNally College Publishing, 1978), pp. 179-185.

that the student can select his own notetaking style.

5. Notes should indicate the original sources used. Therefore, complete bibliographic information about the source read or speaker heard should appear in the notes.
6. Taking notes should not be the end result of an assignment. These notes should be the means by which a student can later return to ideas read or heard and utilize the material.

OUTLINING. To outline, the student identifies and records the main ideas and supporting details of a topic. He records them in the sequence they occurred in the reading or listening activity. The outline should clearly differentiate between the main ideas and details that support them. An outline format can be used as the student takes notes from a selected source or, after the student has taken notes, an outline can be created to organize the material into a form that he can later use.

The two main types of outlines are sentence outlines and topic outlines. The *sentence outline* states each idea in complete sentences. Whereas, the *topic outline* has the student formulate these ideas into words and phrases. More thought is required in the development of a topic outline, as the student must take the sentences in which these ideas were expressed and convert them into key words and phrases for later use.

Outlining involves the utilization of these skills:

1. As with notetaking, a purpose should be set prior to a reading or listening experience so that the resulting outline can include those points necessary to the completion of the reading task.
2. The student should recognize main ideas, key supporting details, and subordinate details.
3. The student must determine the logical sequence in which these ideas should be recorded for later recall.
4. The student should develop a systematic approach to outline development. The procedure should be to first locate the main ideas of a topic. The student will then go back to each main idea and add major supporting details followed by subordinate ones.
5. The relative importance of an idea is indicated in an outline by letter or number and indentation. The same style number or letter and indentation indicates ideas of equal importance (i.e. main ideas are delineated by capital letters, supporting details are in-

dented and numbered, subordinate details are indented and preceded by lowercase letters.) Normally, a passage is not subdivided unless there are at least two ideas of equal importance to be designated in the outline.

6. The student should first learn to create a sentence outline, then a topic or word outline. However, in teaching either type, the teacher should provide a model of a complete outline. Early practice tools should be outlines that have been partially completed by the teacher for the student to complete. As the student becomes more adept, more information can be deleted until he can independently create an outline without teacher assistance.
7. After the student has mastered outlining, he should choose the form of outlining that is the most efficient for him. As with note-taking, outlining is a *means to an end.* It serves to recall ideas previously read or heard and is a tool for the student's individual use.

SUMMARIZING. To summarize, the student gathers and restates the main ideas of a topic read or heard. As with the previously discussed organizational skills, the student must easily recognize main ideas and details and rewrite them in a logical order for later understanding.

Summaries vary as to their length and purpose. Sentences should be brief, to the point, and few in number. Needless words and irrelevant sentences are omitted in a summary.

As with other skills, mastery of summarizing is a developmental process. The student should first be exposed to a single sentence which he summarizes in a word or phrase. Secondly, he should summarize a paragraph by composing a sentence that expresses its main idea. The student should then summarize into a paragraph the key ideas expressed in several paragraphs and, finally, those from a complete reading or discussion.

To reinforce correct choice of main ideas and details, teachers should first illustrate the summarizing process by summarizing a paragraph or sentence for the student. Secondly, the teacher can have the student summarize sections of their textbook or other reading sources that include a summary by the author. Upon completion of his summary, the student would then double-check his choice of statements with those contained in the author's summary.

SYNTHESIZING. Synthesizing is a complex organizational skill that should not be expected of a student until he has had experience in creating summaries. Synthesizing requires the student to organize in a logical order the information about a topic from several sources.

This skill involves essentially the same processes as does summarizing. However, it is more complex by the use of several sources. The student must: (1) read or listen, comprehend, and summarize the main ideas from each source, (2) compare the information learned from the various sources, (3) sequence these ideas in a logical manner with the deletion of redundant ideas, and (4) synthesize these ideas into a writing in his own words.

As with summarizing, synthesizing involves a multi-stepped learning process. The student should first synthesize main ideas from several one-paragraph passages and proceed gradually until he can synthesize information from several lengthy selections.

Synthesizing is especially important to the secondary student who is expected to complete lengthy research projects. By outlining or taking notes on the materials read, the student can work on such a project over a period of time. By later using these written reminders of the content of each selection, he can formulate a final outline for the synthesis of the information obtained.

Flexibility in Reading Rates

Reading rate is the pace at which one reads and comprehends. Rapid reading is of little consequence if comprehension does not result.

Through the selection of appropriate reading rates, reading that results in no comprehension is eliminated. To become flexible in his choice of reading rates, a student must become adept in the skills of skimming, study reading, and scanning. Appropriate use of these rates allows the reader to adjust his reading speed to: (1) the purpose set for reading, (2) the difficulty of the reading material, (3) the time allowed for reading, and (4) the motivation and experiences he brings to the written page.

Skimming is the reading rate a student should use when he first approaches a written selection. He skims when he quickly reads a passage for a general overview, review, or identification of an organizational pattern. If the student develops the habit of first skimming a passage, he can then better concentrate on working to fulfill his reading purpose. As he keeps in mind why he is to read the passage, he can note its general features and determine how the passage should be read to best fulfill his needs. After the passage has been reread slowly and the purpose examined in conjunction with the information learned, the reader can then skim to review the passage to see that he has captured all key ideas.

Study/reading is the rate used after the material has been skimmed. With the reading purpose set so that the student knows how the passage is to be studied, he study/reads to determine all major points and details as they relate to his purpose. Too often this rate is the only one developed by students, and this exclusive use of study/reading often results in little lasting comprehension. Study/reading is only effective if the reader: (1) becomes familiar with his reading purpose, (2) skims the passage to determine patterns and general information, (3) reflects on the reading purpose again with the format of the passage in mind, and (4) study/reads the passage with the fulfillment of his reading purpose as his goal.

After the reader skims and study/reads a passage, he adjusts his rate to *scanning*. This quick reading is to find the answer to a question or to locate a specific fact or idea. Frequently, a reading purpose has as a final activity oral questioning, writing a report or outline, or answering written questions. Scanning allows the reader to quickly glance over a passage to locate the information that specifically fits his reading need. If the reader has been flexible in his reading approach to this point, the efforts he has put into his reading will often help him recall where an idea was located. Therefore, scanning becomes an even more expedient rate than if these first steps had been eliminated from the reading process.

The use of these various reading rates may sound difficult and time consuming. However, students must be convinced that the use of these rates saves time and increases comprehension. More than with other reading/study skills, the use of flexible reading rates must become a habit. A flexible rate should become an automatic reflex without thought.

Graphic Aids

Writers supplement and clarify their writings by the use of

graphic aids. Most commonly these aids include *pictures, graphs, tables, charts*, and *maps*.[10] Subject matter often dictates the type of aids used. For too many readers, these aids merely occupy space. Yet, for the reader struggling with the content of a passage, a graphic aid, especially a captioned picture, can often clarify information that he previously did not understand. Likewise, the more able reader can obtain a more comprehensive understanding of the subject matter by analyzing an accompanying graphic aid.

To increase the use of graphic aids while reading, the teacher must gear instruction so that the students will recognize and understand the skills necessary to interpret each graphic aid. As with any other learning activity, a student will shy away from tasks that frustrate him. Also, he is not likely to use an aid if he is not aware of its benefits to his reading/study efforts. Only if the teacher consistently makes the information contained in these various aids a part of the reading assignment will the use of graphic aids become a natural part of the student's reading.

Pictures, as a graphic aid, are only limited by the teacher's creative use of them in instruction. They can open a new world to the student who has not experienced the event illustrated or they can help the student compare the familiar with the unknown. A pictorial description can also clarify a difficult concept or stress the main idea expressed by the writer.

The forms that pictures can take are endless. For example, *photography* offers a realistic view of people, places, and events, whereas *cartoons* enhance the critical and creative opinions expressed in a written selection.

Through *graphs*, the student compares written information to a visual representation of this information. It is through this visual aid that quantitative information is organized as a concise summary. The primary types of graphs are *picture, bar, line*, and *circle graphs*. Graphs are most beneficial in the areas of mathematics, science, and social sciences.

Picture graphs use pictures to compare quantities or items (e.g. one car could equal 1,000 cars manufactured within a given year). Pic-

---

[10]Graphic aids and ideas discussed about each are based on graphic aids discussed in Cooper, J. David et al.: *The What and How of Reading Instruction* (Columbus: Merrill, 1979), pp. 162-174.

ture graphs are single-axis graphs.[11] Ease in reading makes them a popular choice. Their major disadvantage is that it is difficult to indicate a portion of a quantity represented. Only an estimation of a portion of the whole picture can be used to illustrate a representative amount on the graph. For example, in the ilustration, 300 cars would be represented by a portrayal of one-third of a whole car.

Vertical or horizontal lines are used to compare quantities in a *bar graph*. The bar graph is a two-axis graph with each variable represented by a separate line. These graphs can be utilized to compare sizes of separate objects (e.g., height of various breeds of dogs) or to compare the change that occurs to a singular object (e.g. height of a specific child at each year of his life).

Line graphs show progress or changes in amounts over a period of time. This graph is a two-axis graph with vertical or horizontal scales with each indicating a value for a point plotted on the line (e.g. the number of home runs hit by a baseball player over a 6-year period).

The *circle graph*, the easiest of the graphs to read, allows comparison of a part to the whole. As the name implies, this graph is not built on an axis but is in the form of a circle. It best indicates the percentage of a whole (100%) that an item represents (e.g. a whole circle could indicate people who smoke with each portion of the circle representing the percentage of a particular group that smokes compared to the whole).

Another graphic means to organize data for comparison is through *tables and charts*. Although easy to adapt to various subject areas, tables and charts are often difficult for students to comprehend. Students can be frustrated by the great number of words and corresponding figures that must be interpreted.

Tables and charts are organized by means of vertical and horizontal columns. Multiple or singular columns may be used. Without first skimming the table or chart to determine its main purpose and key categories, the student cannot successfully analyze data shown within it. Thus, the student must first read and comprehend the title of the table or chart and the titles of each division therein. These orient him to the focus of the graphic aid, and he can then determine the sub-

[11]An *axis* is the horizontal or vertical line that runs along the edge of the graph and is the basis of each graph, except a circle graph.

categories into which the data is analyzed. An example would be a chart entitled *Helpers* with the vertical subdivisions showing the days of the week and the horizontal lines containing the names of various students. A student can use this information to focus on a particular day of the week to determine who the helper is that day, or he can locate the name of a particular student to see on which day he helps.

Maps are found in almost all social studies materials. They are flat representations of the features of an area. A map can be comprehensive in nature (e.g. represent the whole world) or can feature one particular aspect of an area portrayed (e.g. rainfall or population).

To correlate map reading with the reading of a textbook, the student should develop these skills and habits:

1. *Title of map*. The student should skim the map to locate its title. Commonly, the title is at the top of a map, but it can also be found below the map in the form of a heading for the map's legend or key. Once found, the student should analyze the title to determine the area and features depicted. This information indicates the map's purpose. The reader then can compare the map's purpose with his reading goals to determine the function that the map will play in his reading and learning activities.
2. *Types of maps*. The student should be familiar with the types of maps he will encounter in his reading. Included in these are political and physical maps as well as globes which are spherical representations of the world's surface.
3. *Use of symbols*. The student must be aware that symbols represent the features or attributes portrayed by a map (e.g. an airplane symbolizes an airport). This awareness leads the student to the legend of the map where the various symbols are explained.
4. *Scale*. A part of the key or legend is the map's scale. The student must realize that a map cannot be drawn the same size of the area it represents; thus, all maps are reduced. To determine the actual distance between two points, the scale is used to indicate the specific measure representing a distance on the map (e.g. 1 inch equals 1,000 miles).
5. *Direction*. The reader must determine directions (North, South, East, West) on the map in order to locate certain points in relation to their directional lie. Although some maps differ, most

show North at the top, South at the bottom, East to the right, and West to the left. The location of these directions should be determined prior to the location of a specific point on the map. Upon the students' mastery of these four directions and their abbreviations, the intermediate directions (i.e. Southeast, Northeast, Southwest, Northwest) should be taught.

6. *Lines of Latitude and Longitude*. Knowledge of these lines are often necessary to locate a point on a map. These imaginary lines aid in location by the use of coordinates (degrees) of *latitude* and *longitude*. The *latitudinal lines* run parallel to each other in an east to west direction. Also called *parallels*, they indicate distances north to south of the equator with the equator being the zero parallel.

   The *longitudinal lines* run in a north and south direction and meet at the poles. Also called *meridians*, they represent distances east to west of the zero meridian.

   A *degree* (°) is the unit of measure that shows the distance between lines of latitude and longitude. A degree can be broken into sixty parts, referred to as minutes ('). Therefore, the measure of a distance of latitude or longitude is stated as a point *X* degrees, *Y* minutes (e.g. 30°15') from a specific location.
7. *Critical/inferential map reading*. Once the student has learned how to utilize a map, he should then be placed in a variety of activities that incorporate reading with map use. He should be required to critically analyze the contents of a map as well as to infer ideas suggested by the map in conjunction with the reading.

Principles of Reading/Study Skills Instruction

Reading/study skills instruction includes a wide range of skills and areas of study. Whereas, the teaching of word recognition and comprehension skills primarily occurs in the reading classroom, the development and use of reading/study skills takes place in both reading and content-area situations. Thus, one must first determine how reading/study skills can best be taught before actual instruction.

The teacher must be aware of the structure of each reading/study skill as each skill is composed of several subskills. For example, in using the dictionary, the student must alphabetize, decode, and compare definitions. Therefore, if a teacher is to require students to use reading/study skills, she must be certain that she: (1) recognizes the components of each skill, (2) sees that the students have sufficiently mastered each of the subskills required in the application of the reading/study skill, and (3) teaches the students the step-by-step process that must be followed to implement the reading/study skill in their reading assignments. If a student is having difficulty with the use of a reading/study skill, the teacher should first analyze the student's understanding of the several subskills that make up that skill. His misuse of one of these component skills may prevent him from effectively using the reading/study skill.

As suggested, reading/study skills can be taught both in the reading and content-area classrooms. The emphasis of the remainder of this section and the section on "Classroom Applications" will be on the integration of reading/study skills into the content-area classroom. The suggestions made in this section can, however, be easily adapted to the reading classroom.

Teach, Practice, Apply

As mentioned earlier, reading/study skills should be introduced to students through the use of materials to be studied. The students should recognize them to be an integral part of their study techniques and not isolated skills that in no way aid in their comprehension of the reading materials.

When presenting a reading/study skill, the teacher should first *teach* the students the mechanics of the skill as it is to be used in learning situations in the classroom. During this aspect of instruction, the teacher should *walk through* the process with the students so that they: (1) see the purpose of the skill, (2) understand its actual application to the content-area materials, (3) know the written/verbal response expected of them when using the skill, and (4) learn the expected results of their efforts.

After the skill has been introduced, the student should have varied opportunities to *practice* the use of the newly learned skill in his study of the content-area materials. These practice sessions should be guided by the teacher. In the first stages, the teacher and student should work together step by step. Then, the student can independently work through an exercise. When he completes the exercise, the teacher can evaluate the results. Finally, the student can revise his work if necessary. This practice allows the student to: (1) think through the process, (2) see the correct application, and (3) immediately correct and learn from his mistakes. Practice should continue until the student has mastered the mechanics of the skill in its application to the content-area materials in use.

Finally, upon mastery of the skill, the student will *apply* the skill to the reading/study materials through daily reading assignments. The goal of this three-step process (teach, practice, apply) is to enable the student to become an independent learner. The student should be able to retain and understand content-area concepts and carry these newly learned concepts to future learning and real-life situations. If the student cannot independently use a reading/study skill, additional practice time should be allowed.[12]

Readability of Reading Selections

The readability of a reading selection greatly determines a student's successful use of that material and determines pertinent learning activities. *Readability* is the reading difficulty of a written selection. The level at which a material is written, the material's format, the reading level of the student, the student's proposed use of the material, and his interest in the reading all directly relate to the readability of the selection.

The reading level of a passage is easily determined through the use of a *readability formula*. This formula determines the selection's level of difficulty by an analysis of sentence length and vocabulary difficulty. Longer sentences and more difficult vocabulary make the reading passage more difficult to read.

Various formulas are available for teachers to use in the analysis of their textbooks, supplementary sources, written activities and tests. One such readability formula is the *Raygor Reading Estimate*[13] Its administrative ease and speed make it a favorable choice for teachers.

To implement the Raygor Reading Estimate, three 100-word passages are selected. The passages represent selections from the beginning, middle, and end of the reading material being analyzed. Within this 100-word count are included proper nouns (e.g. Phyllis)

[12]The process of *teach, practice, apply* is also applicable to the reading/study strategies discussed in a later section.

[13]Based on Raygor, A.L.: *The Raygor Readability Estimate: A Quick and Easy Way to Determine Difficulty*. Paper presented at National Reading Conference, 1976.

but not numerals (e.g. 66). After the passages are selected, the formula is applied to each passage. First, the sentences within a passage are counted, estimating the last, incomplete sentence (if applicable) to the nearest tenth. Secondly, words are counted within the passage that have six or more letters. (The authors suggest circling these words for easier counting.) The process is then repeated for the remaining two selected passages.

After completing the steps above, the number of sentences found in the three passages are averaged together. Next, the number of six-letter words from the three passages are averaged. These two averages are then used to plot on the graph the average reading level of the written material.

The authors suggest that the above-mentioned process can be varied to determine if the reading source is *consistent* in its reading level throughout the source rather than determining the average reading level of the entire source. To do so, the reading level of *each* individual passage is plotted by using its individual number of sentences and number of words with six or more letters. This process is repeated for each of the three passages. These three levels are then compared to see if they are similar.[14]

After the teacher has applied a readability formula to a reading source to determine its level of difficulty, she must then compare the results to her proposed use of the material in the classroom. The factors she must consider are these: (1) the format of the material, (2) how the student will be expected to use the source, (3) the reading level of the student, and (4) the student's attitude toward the material.

Most importantly, the teacher must compare the reading level of the source with the reading level of the students. To compare the two, the teacher must be aware of the independent, instructional,

[14]A reading source would be considered to have consistent readability if the first passage was found to be at the sixth-grade reading level, the middle one at the sixth-grade level, and the final one at the fifth-grade reading level. These results would indicate that the reading level of the entire text would probably fall between the fifth- and sixth-grade reading levels. However, a teacher should be wary of a reading source in which the reading level of the first passage falls at the fifth-grade level, the middle passage at the ninth-grade level, and the final passage at the seventh-grade level. These latter findings would possibly indicate that the writer did not consider reading levels in his writing, and the source could not be used with a student reading below the ninth-grade reading level.

THE RAYGOR READABILITY ESTIMATE

ALTON L. RAYGOR - UNIVERSITY OF MINNESOTA

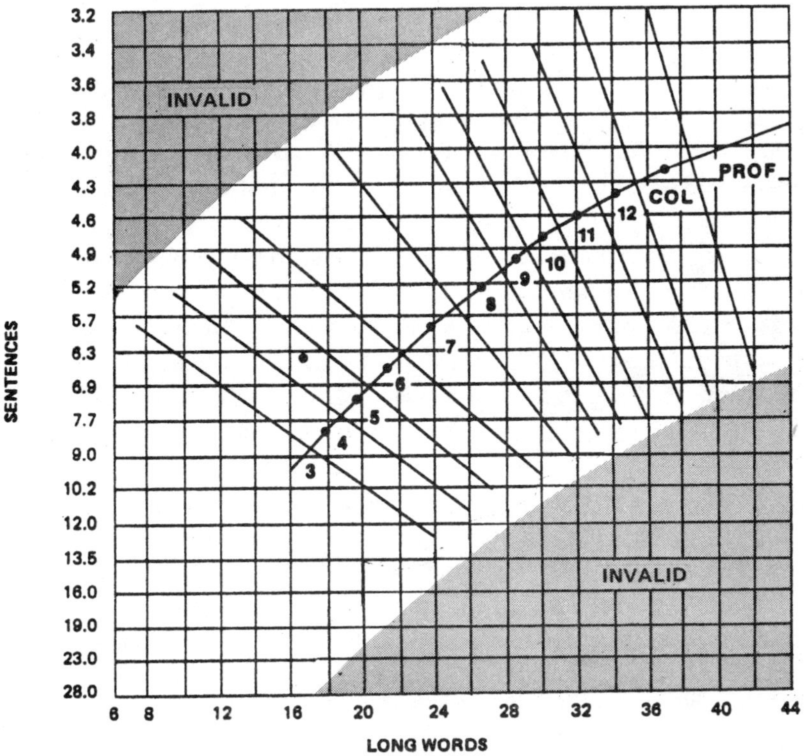

Directions:

Count out three 100-word passages near the beginning, middle, and end of a selection or book. Count proper nouns, but not numerals.

1. Count sentences in each passage, estimating to nearest tenth.
2. Count words with six or more letters.
3. Average the sentence length and word length over the three samples and plot the average on the graph.

Example:

	Sentences	*6+ Words*
A	6.0	15
B	6.8	19
C	6.4	17
Total	19.2	51
Average	6.4	17

Note mark on graph. Grade level is about 5.

and frustrational reading levels of the students.[15] This information can be obtained from school records or the administration of an informal reading inventory.

Knowledge of her students' reading levels combined with the use of a readability formula gives the teacher a quick indication of which sources to use in the classroom and which sources to avoid. Moreover, depending on the availability of textbooks at the necessary reading levels, the teacher can see how to structure classroom instruction.

Comparing the reading level of the students with the readability level of reading materials is only the starting point in determining how well students can be expected to use a particular source. Other extraneous factors can enhance or hamper a book's readability for the students. One such factor is the book's format: the size and type of print, spacing between lines of print, use of headings and graphic aids, and the placement of each in relation to the reading matter. Additionally, the students' attitudes toward the subject matter and the purposes set for the reading material also aid in the determination of whether a source should be utilized as a teaching tool.

Readability of written materials can be brought to the attention of the student by providing him with a commonsense approach for selecting independent reading sources. He should build the habit of flipping through a selection to examine its format and the ease with which he can follow the reading on a page. A student should skim a short passage at the beginning, middle, and end of the selection. If he has difficulty with a large number of words that prevent him from understanding what he read, the source is too difficult and

---

[15]The *independent level* is the reading level at which the student can read a source without any guidance and can understand and apply the ideas read. Word recognition and comprehension of the material pose no problem for the student. The *instructional level* is the level at which a student can read the source with teacher aid. He may have some difficulty with word recognition and comprehension; however, the difficulty can be overcome with the teacher's assistance. The third level is the student's *frustrational reading level*. The student should not be expected to read a source written at this level. His vocabulary difficulties prevent an understanding of the ideas and concepts contained in the material. Therefore, for the reader who reads independently at the eighth-grade level, instructionally at the tenth-grade level, and frustrationally at the eleventh-grade level, the teacher should make independent reading assignments in materials written at the eighth-grade level or below. With teacher guidance, the student could be expected to use a source written on the ninth- or tenth-grade level but could not be expected to use a source written on the eleventh-grade level or above.

another should be chosen. Teachers, however, should be aware that when students first begin to make their own selections, they will often choose materials that are more difficult than they can handle. Some students find it necessary to show their peers and the teacher that they can and want to read a more difficult book. Telling the student he cannot possibly read a book he selected will only add to his determination. In time, if left alone, the student will *self-adjust* his selection process.

The same holds true for the student who chooses an *easy-to-read* selection when he could be reading materials written at a higher reading level. In time, he will probably choose materials that more closely resemble his independent/instructional reading level. Only when the selection of inappropriate materials continues over a long period of time should the teacher intervene.

The principles of readability also apply to testing materials and other written exercises. If a large portion of students do poorly on a test, the teacher should check the readability of the instrument. The test may be written at a level that the students cannot read. The teacher must determine whether she is testing reading ability or knowledge of content-area concepts.

APPLICATION OF READING/STUDY SKILLS

These exercises provide the reader with the opportunity to utilize the reading/study skills presented in this chapter.

Barbara is seeking a position as a librarian. She has learned that she must submit a *resume*.

1. What general topic in a reference source would Barbara look up to see what the purpose of a *resume* is in her attempts to obtain this position? She has looked under resume but did not find sufficient information.
2. Barbara cannot pronounce *resume*. What reference source would she use to determine its pronunciation?
3. If Barbara wanted to find additional books on this topic in the library, which of the three types of cards in the card catalog would she use?
4. Barbara found four sources that would aid her in her re-

search. She had to choose one. Listed below are the pagings of the four sources. Which would be the most helpful?

a. 112-113 c. 91

b. 160-169 d. 81-84

5. Barbara would like to find a job in a large, coastal city in the United States. Locate on a map of the United States five cities in which Barbara would search for a job.

6. Using the *Reader's Guide to Periodical Literature*, locate an article on *job hunting*. What is the main idea of this article. Tell how you determined this idea to be the main idea.

7. Using a topic outline, outline the main ideas and supporting details of this periodical article.

8. Summarize this article into one paragraph.

9. Using one of the graphic aids suggested in this chapter, design one to complement a major aspect of this article.

10. Locate the topic used to answer exercise 1. Synthesize this passage with the periodical article located in answer to exercise 6.

11. Using the Raygor Readability Estimate, determine the reading level of the two articles used in exercise 10. Keeping in mind the three levels of reading (independent, instructional and frustrational), how would you use these articles with Sam who reads instructionally at the ninth-grade level; Jimmy who reads instructionally at the sixth-grade level; and Tonya who reads on a second-grade level?

CLASSROOM APPLICATIONS

As earlier noted, reading/study skills instruction occurs in both reading and content-area classrooms. When the main emphasis is on the content area itself, the concepts and ideas of the content area are of utmost importance and not the teaching of reading/study skills. These skills should be viewed as a *means to an end* to enhance comprehension of the concepts of the content area. Thus, reading/study skills instruction must be correlated to the study of the content materials. Coverage of concepts and ideas should not be interrupted for isolated, unrelated practice of reading/study skills through the use of activities that do not pertain to the content area. Instead, skill instruction must be intertwined, with the content material serving as a stimulus for skill instruction.

Thus, the procedures used to introduce reading/study skills revolve around materials used, learning requirements, reading level of the students and the students' previous exposure, and use of reading/study skills in that particular area of study. Suggestions made for teaching reading/study skills must, therefore, be adapted to the area taught and to the students involved in the learning.

Reading/Study Strategies

Reading/study strategies, when used in conjunction with reading/study skills, greatly enhance content-area learning. These strategies are individually designed to provide students with a quick, specialized approach to reading in the various content areas. Each of the strategies discussed below is designed to meet the reading demands of a particular area. Each can be used as written or adapted to fit individual needs.

As with any other instructional technique, the student must be convinced that his learning will be improved and time will be saved through the use of this strategy. He must also be given time to practice the strategy in order to become proficient in its use.

SQ3R

SQ3R,[16] most commonly associated with social studies, can readily be adapted to most content-area subjects. Its use enables the student to find the main ideas of topics read. The steps of this strategy are these:

1. *Survey*. The student first quickly skims chapter title, boldfaced headings, summary paragraphs, and graphic aids. This overview provides the student with a general scheme of the organization of the passage, main ideas, and important details.

2. *Question*. Through the use of purpose-setting questions suggested by the author and the formulation of questions from chapter headings and subheadings, the student determines his purpose for reading.

3. *Read*. The student now reads to answer the questions he

[16]Robinson, F.: *Effective Study*, 4th ed. (New York: Harper & Row, 1970), pp. 31-32.

formed in the prior step. This process enables him to read with a purpose. Notes can be taken.

4. *Recite*. Without the aid of book or notes, the student answers the questions earlier formed and determined through his reading.

5. *Review*. The student verifies his answers to the questions through his notes and the selection read.

SQRQCQ

Mathematical *word problems* (also referred to as thought problems and story problems) present a difficulty for many students. Even those with no mathematical deficiencies can frequently not work through the demands of such problems. The cause is that often these students cannot *read* the problem to carry out the necessary mathematical operations. Use of the strategies, SQRQCQ,[17] can help eliminate this problem. To implement this strategy, these steps are followed:

1. *Survey*. The student skims the problem for a general overview of its purpose.

2. *Question*. The student then questions himself as to the problem's specific purpose. He should ask the question, "What does the problem ask me to do?"

3. *Read*. The problem is then slowly reread. Close attention should be given to essential details and relationships.

4. *Question*. The student must now decide what mathematical operations are necessary for the word problem to be completed. If more than one operation is required, he should also determine the order in which each of these operations should be performed. He should ask himself, "What type of mathematical procedure(s) must I follow? Which should be completed first, second, etc.?"

5. *Compute*. Using the above-mentioned procedures in their correct order, the student now computes the answer to the problem.

6. *Question*. The student scans the problem, the procedure(s) used, and the answer to see if he is correct. He should ask, "Does the answer make sense? If not, have I chosen the correct procedures and properly completed them?"

---

[17]Fay, L.: Reading study skills in math and science. *Reading and Inquiry*. (Newark: International Reading Association, 1965), pp. 93-94.

PQRST

Science materials require a more exact reading than do most other content areas. Often, the student is required to draw conclusions based on scientific data. To do so, he is required to be aware of step-by-step processes and their relationship to the ideas discussed. PQRST[18] is the study strategy designed to aid in the reading of science materials. The steps are these:

1. *Preview.* By skimming the passage, the student determines the nature of the reading.

2. *Question.* He then poses questions from the passage's main headings and subheadings. These questions set the purpose for the student's reading.

3. *Read.* With these questions in mind, the student now studies/reads the passage. He determines all major ideas that relate to his reading purpose.

4. *Summarize.* The student summarizes in paragraph or listing form the main thoughts of the reading. Often, this summary takes the form of a step-by-step analysis of a scientific process discussed.

6. *Test.* Without the aid of the textbook or summary, the student asks himself the questions posed earlier in this strategy. If he cannot recall the answers without assistance, he should review the steps of this strategy to clarify his understanding.

EVOKER

EVOKER[19] is the study strategy designed for reading literary selections such as poetry, prose and drama. It stresses the expressive oral reading of a passage as well as its overall meaning. The procedure used is as follows:

1. *Explore.* The entire passage is read silently to obtain a *feeling* for the passage.

2. *Vocabulary.* The passage is then examined for unknown key words. Often, these writings include people, places, and events that are foreign to the student. A clear understanding of these words is essential for the student to gain the full meaning of the passage. He

---

[18] Spache, G.: *Toward Better Reading* (Champaign: Garrard, 1963), p. 94.

[19] Pauk, W.: On scholarship: advice to high school students. *The Reading Teacher*, 17: 73, 78.

should, moreover, locate certain words in the dictionary for their correct pronunciation if he does not know how to pronounce them.

3. *Oral Reading*. At this point, the passage is read orally. It should be read several times so that the student can read it with as much expression as possible.

4. *Key Ideas*. The student should note the main theme or ideas of the selection so he can better understand the writer's organization of the passage.

5. *Evaluation*. To determine if the student has correctly defined unfamiliar words and understood key sentences, these should be compared with the main idea determined in the preceding step.

6. *Recapitulation*. The selection is reread again, both orally and silently, so that the student can fully appreciate the meaning and expression of the passage.

Testing Procedures

Most content-area teachers conclude a unit of study by testing the students' understanding of concepts and materials covered in the study. The planning and preparation for tests should be the same as for the use of reading/study skills in the content area. The teacher should teach the students how to prepare for a test, follow test directions, and complete the instrument itself. The testing instrument should reflect the concepts studied and require the students to utilize only those skills demanded of them in the classroom situation.

The testing of a completed assignment, chapter, or unit of study should be constructed with these factors in mind:[20]

1. The test should directly reflect information taught.
2. Skills required during classroom activities should be the type of skills used in the completion of the test.
3. The test should be written on the reading level of the students. If too difficult, it should be read to the student.
4. Directions should be written as well as discussed orally. The students who learn primarily by listening will have the opportunity to hear the directions. Additionally, the visual learner will also have a chance to see the directions in written form.

---

[20]Woodington, C.C. and Perry, L.A.: *Teaching the Reading Teachers* (Springfield: Thomas, 1983), pp. 142-143.

5. The test should not be a shock to the students. They should be familiar with the techniques. A teacher should teach by one approach and use that same approach on related tests.

6. The teacher should provide the students with immediate feedback of test results so they can learn from their errors.

7. If a majority of students do poorly on a test, the teacher needs to check the reading level of the test as well as the items stressed on it and those presented in class. More than likely the teacher needs to repeat instruction so that the students will better understand. The goal of the content-area teacher is not test scores; it is student understanding.

READING/STUDY SKILLS POSTTEST

1. Name four types of *dictionaries* and describe their use.
2. What should the content-area teacher never assume about the students' ability to use reading/study skills in the classroom? Why?
3. What is the *Reader's Guide to Periodical Literature*?
4. What bibliographic information is found on the *title page* of a book?
5. Define *lines of latitude* and *lines of longitude*.
6. How should a teacher incorporate a textbook's *graphic aids* into a reading assignment? List three graphic aids.
7. Define *readability*. Explain how a teacher determines the readability of a textbook for her class.
8. Which is more difficult, *summarizing* or *synthesizing*? Why?
9. Discuss the purpose of the major *organizational patterns* that structure reading passages. What is a *signal word* for each?
10. What is the purpose of *notetaking* as a reading/study skill?
11. When does a student use *selection skills*?
12. Why must a student know how to *alphabetize* to locate a reading selection?
13. Define *legend* in terms of a map skill. What is usually found in a map's legend?
14. How does a *circle graph* differ from other graphs?
15. Define *content-area instruction*.
16. List the skills involved in locating a supplementary reading

source in the library and then locating the necessary passage within the selected source(s).

17. How does the reader locate the *main idea* and its *supporting details* in a reading passage?
18. What are three ways to use the *card catalog* to locate a book in the library?
19. Define *teach, practice, apply*. What is its purpose in the content-area classroom?
20. Why should reading/study skills be emphasized in the content-area classroom?
21. What factors should a teacher consider in constructing a test for content-area use?
22. List four factors a teacher should consider when selecting a textbook for content-area instruction.
23. Explain the use of an *encyclopedia* in a content-area classroom.
24. List the steps a teacher should follow in teaching students how to *outline*.
25. Why should a content-area teacher be concerned about teaching reading/study skills to her class?
26. Define *atlas*. Why is it important in social studies instruction?
27. Discuss how each of these rates are used by a reader who is flexible in his reading: *skimming, study/reading, scanning*.
28. Define the role that *reading/study strategies* play in content-area instruction.
29. Discuss the steps a reader goes through to locate a topic in a reference source.
30. Discuss the five major *reading/study skills* for use in the content areas.
31. What *map skills* are needed by a student to enable him to use a map when reading a textbook?

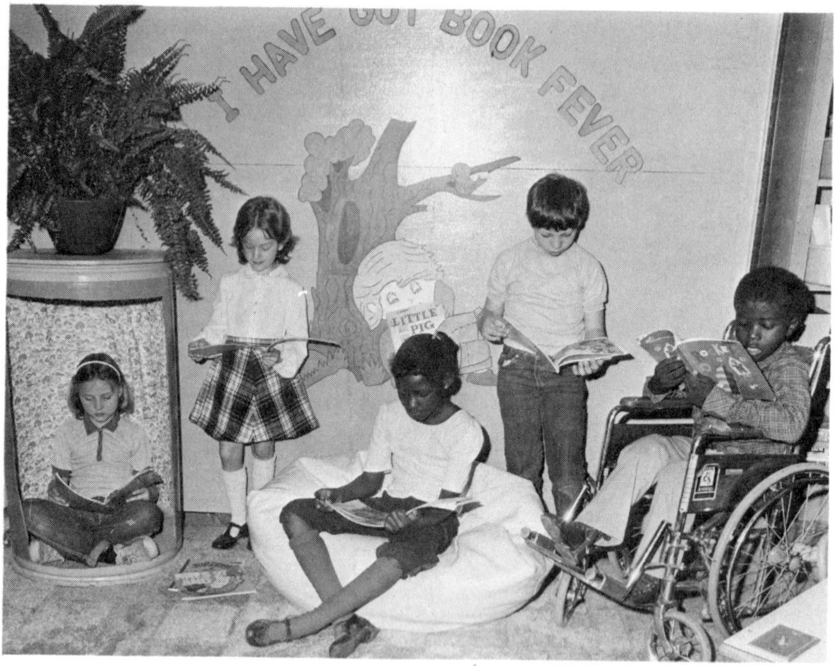
I HAVE GOT BOOK FEVER
LITTLE PIG

CHAPTER 7

READING INTERESTS AND APPRECIATION

THE final chapter of *Teaching Basic Skills in Reading* discusses ways of developing reading interests and appreciation. Reading instruction is not complete if it focuses only on the development of reading skills. Students also need to acquire an interest in and appreciation of a variety of types of written materials.

The reader can use the following pretest to assess his/her prior knowledge of the topics presented in Chapter 7.

PRETEST

1. What is the strongest motivating factor on student reading?
2. What are some alternatives to written book reports?
3. How can the physical environment of a classroom affect a stu-

dent's desire to engage in voluntary reading?
4. What is a *book display* and how can it be used to promote reading as a leisure-time activity?
5. How can a teacher make use of an *interest inventory*?
6. With whom should students compete in *book contests*?
7. From what sources can a teacher obtain books for the classroom reading center?
8. How can television have a positive influence on reading?
9. What types of books can be included in the classroom collection?
10. In what way does the emotional climate of a classroom influence student reading?
11. Why does reading aloud to students encourage them to read independently?
12. What is *reading appreciation*?

DEFINITION AND IMPORTANCE OF READING INTERESTS AND APPRECIATION

The phrase *reading interests and appreciation* refers to several aspects of reading development. *Reading interests* are those subjects about which students have a desire to read. However, reading interests can also refer to an interest in reading itself. For those students who simply have no desire to read about anything, an interest in reading must be developed.

Traditionally, *reading appreciation* has referred to an appreciation of *good* works of literature, such as the classics. In this chapter, however, the term has been expanded to include an appreciation of many types of written materials and an appreciation, or value, of reading itself.

As students become acquainted with different types of literature such as fiction, nonfiction, poetry, etc., they will also be exposed to a variety of styles of writing. They should learn to appreciate the writing style of various authors as they become aware of the way different authors use words to convey their message.

As was previously stated, reading instruction that focuses only on the development of reading skills is inadequate. The goal in reading instruction should be to produce students who *can and do read*. If a student has mastered all the basic reading skills but never reads anything independently, he is certin to *lose ground*. Reading growth occurs primarily through wide reading.

Wide reading involves reading at times other than the period set aside for reading instruction during the school day. It involves reading more than the basal reader. Teachers need to foster in their students a *love of reading* so that they will voluntarily choose reading as a leisure-time activity.

Whether they read for pleasure or the acquisition of information, those students who are motivated to engage in voluntary reading will automatically expand their reading skills. Students should also be encouraged to develop a *lifelong reading habit* so that they can continue to enjoy the benefits of reading after their years of formal schooling have ended.

Finally, in the mid 1980s there exist many demands for a student's time. Television, video games, and other forms of *instant entertainment* are very appealing to most of today's students. However, the book is the only truly portable source of both information and pleasure. A book can be read practically anywhere, anytime with no additional equipment or special adaptors. Teachers must develop in their students an interest in and appreciation of this valuable form of communication and entertainment.

DEVELOPING READING INTERESTS AND APPRECIATION

In the following sections three aspects of developing reading interests and appreciation will be discussed: the teacher's role, interest inventories, and materials for independent reading.

The Teacher's Role

The teacher's role in developing reading interests and appreciation consists mainly of providing motivation and a supportive environment. One of the strongest motivating factors on student reading is a teacher's enthusiasm about reading and books. If the teacher is enthusiastic about reading, her students will sense this and they too will appreciate reading as a worthwhile activity.

Teachers who regularly read to their students communicate their enthusiasm for reading. Students often want to read a book that their teacher has read to them. Hearing a book read aloud also allows students to enjoy a book that may be too difficult for them to read independently.

Some teachers read selected portions of a book to their students, thereby motivating the students to read the entire book on their own. Storytelling also encourages students to read as they seek out the books on which the stories were based.

Setting aside class time for voluntary reading is another way to motivate students to read widely. When the teacher also reads during this time, she becomes a positive *role model*. If the students see their teacher read for pleasure or read to obtain information, they are likely to want to imitate her actions.

Just as some teacher actions can effect positive attitudes toward reading, other teacher behaviors can produce negative attitudes. If students equate reading with completing workbook pages and ditto sheets, one can easily see how their enthusiasm for reading may be lacking. Students should be given the opportunity to practice their reading skills in actual reading situations and not required to do reading-related activities as *busy work*.

Both the physical and the emotional aspects of the classroom environment can influence a student's desire to engage in voluntary reading. The teacher has a great deal of control over the classroom environment. A classroom that is attractive, functional, and free from unnecessary clutter will make students feel both comfortable and secure. Appropriate room temperature and proper lighting—elements often beyond the control of the teacher—also contribute to the comfort of the students and thereby increase their desire to engage in reading and other learning activities.

A special area of the classroom should be set aside as a classroom reading center. Books should be attractively displayed so that the students can easily select books to read. Comfortable chairs, a section of carpet, or large pillows can be used to provide places for students to sit as they look over books they may want to read. The reading center should not be a place where students can *goof off*, however. It should be a quiet place where positive attitudes toward reading can be developed.

The emotional climate of a classroom is equally as important as the physical aspect. A warm, supportive teacher plays a greater role in student learning than expensive equipment and *fancy* materials. Since students cannot read for pleasure if they cannot read, the teacher who encourages all reading efforts is more likely to produce students who *can and do read*.

Interest Inventories

Students are more likely to read about topics in which they have a special interest. For example, a student who is *crazy about* motorcycles would be much more likely to read a book about motorcycles than a book about flower gardening. However, a student whose parents operate a greenhouse might prefer a book on flower gardening. The challenge to the teacher is to get the *right book* with the *right child*.

Hobbies and leisure-time activities can provide the foundation for many reading interests. A student who is interested in rock collecting can be led to discover exciting and colorful books on rocks and minerals. Many interesting books are available on a variety of hobbies.

A favorite leisure-time activity for many students is watching television. Television provides entertainment without making many demands on the viewer. Rather than bemoan the fact that today's students watch too much television, teachers would do well to capitalize on television interests.

A perceptive teacher can easily transform television interests into reading interests. There can be no doubt that television has expanded the horizons of many students. Through television, students have learned about faraway places they may never have heard about before. They may enjoy reading books about some of these places. Many students watch major sporting events on television. Perhaps they would like to read books about some of these sports and/or sports heros. A quick look through a television program guide can give a teacher an idea of the many reading topics suggested by television shows.

In order to determine her students' interests so that she can *lead them to* books she knows will appeal to them, the teacher can use a questionnaire called an *interest inventory*. In the Appendix are two interest inventories,[1] one for primary students and one for older students.

Materials for Independent Reading

The availability of reading materials influences students' interest in reading. If the only time students get to select books is once a week when they go to the school libary, they will not read as much as they would if books were continually available to them.

Books should be readily available in the classroom. These books might come from the school library, city library, regional bookmobile, used-book store, personal libraries, or the library science department of a nearby university.

The books available to students should cover a wide range of topics and should be at varying levels of difficulty. In other words, there should be *something for everyone*, including interesting books for less-able readers.

Some of the types of books that can be included in a classroom collection are: adventure books, animal books, arts and crafts books, biographies, books about characters with whom students can identify, books bout history and geography, books about real people, books about transportation and communication, fantasies, folk literature (folk tales, fables, myths, etc.), humorous books, mysteries, nonsense books, poetry books, science and nature books, and sports and games books.

In addition to books, the reading center can contain other types of reading materials such as comic books, children's magazines and other periodicals, and travel books from various locations. The wise teacher will not *look down* on a student's choice of reading materials. No book should be considered *inferior* to another. It might be nice if all students selected classics and contemporary classics. (Contemporary classics are those books that have not been around as long as classics but are likely to be considered classics in the future.) However, not all students will have *refined* reading tastes. For a student who never reads anything *on his own*, reading comic books is a good beginning and may lead to more *mature* reading choices.

---

[1] Woodington, C.C. and Perry, L.A.: *Teaching the Reading Teachers* (Springfield: Thomas, 1983), pp. 103-105.

The reading center can also include collections of stories the students have written. Stories written by students can be bound together or placed in looseleaf notebooks so that they can be enjoyed by other students. Also included in the classroom collection can be stories that have been cut from old basal readers and placed in paper covers. Each story can be a separate book that students can complete in a short period of time.

The books in the reading center should be *rotated* periodically. The teacher can put out *new* books and remove books in which the students seem to have little interest. If the students know that new books will be added every two weeks or so, their interest in the reading center's materials can be kept high.

Teacher guidance is necessry if students are to become aware of the wealth of reading materials available. Students should eventually learn, however, how to select appropriate reading materials on their own without teacher assistance. Students who have developed reading interests and an appreciation of reading, and who are able to select appropriate materials independently, are more likely to voluntarily choose reading as a leisure-time activity.

CLASSROOM APPLICATIONS

Presented in this portion of Chapter 7 is a discussion of several classroom applications relating to reading interests and appreciation. The areas discussed are: bulletin boards and displays, book contests, and book report alternatives.

Bulletin Boards and Displays

As was previously mentioned, the classroom environment influences a student's desire to engage in reading and other learning activities. Bulletin boards are an important part of the classroom environment. Attractive, attention-getting bulletin boards can foster reading interests and encourage voluntary reading.

Teacher idea books can be consulted for a variety of ideas for bulletin boards that promote reading. A bulletin board that features, for example, the book jackets of several new books will attract attention to those books and cause students to become interested in reading them. Another bulletin board might revolve around a particular theme, such as volcanoes, and could feature *mock book jackets* of available books on volcanoes. Still another bulletin board might incorporate the titles of books read and enjoyed by various students in the class.

Book displays usually feature a particular type of book, like biographies, or books on a particular theme, such as football. These books can be attractively displayed on a table or shelf in the reading center. Whenever possible, related objects should be displayed with the books as attention-getters. For example, a football and a pair of shoulder pads or a helmet could be displayed with books about football.

Again, television interests should not be overlooked. Pictures of popular television characters can be displayed along with related books. For example, pictures of characters from a television program that involves car chases might be displayed with books about cars or books about how *stunts* are filmed.

Signs or posters, especially those made by the students, can be used as additional attention-getters. Signs with *catchy* slogans can be particularly effective in generating interest in the books featured in a book display. Displays centering around seasons or holidays could be highlighted by slogans such as *Fall into a Good Book* or *Spring into Reading*.

Book Contents

Book contests can be held to encourage students to engage in voluntary reading. Students who reach a predetermined goal can be rewarded with stickers or other tokens reflecting their accomplishment. Caution must be used, however, to assure that less-able readers do not feel *left out*. If students compete with themselves rather than with each other, the negative effects of competition can be avoided.

In one type of book contest where a student competes with himself, each student is given a *bookworm* duplicated on construction paper. The segments of the worm should be drawn large enough so that the student (or teacher) can write in each segment the title of a book that the student read. When the student fills all the segments of the *worm*, he receives some type of reward or privilege. Students of limited ability can read easier books. Thus, each student has a chance for success and no student is left out.

In addition to stickers or other tokens, students can also be given certificates when they have read a specified number of books or given certificates stating how many books they have read. Teachers can create very *official-looking* certificates and duplicate them to give to their students. Rewards of this type motivate students to read even more. They also help students associate reading with something pleasurable (receiving rewards).

As was noted above, the titles of books the students read can be incorporated into a bulletin board to encourage wide reading. These titles could also be written on strips of colored paper (e.g. Anita read *Curious George*). The strips can then be used to form paper chains that can be prominently displayed around the classroom.

Book Report Alternatives

Students who are required to write out a book report for each book they read may end up preferring not to read. In order to keep interest in reading high, teachers must seek alternatives to the traditional written book report.

Many students enjoy sharing a book with classmates. This sharing could take the form of a *book review* or *book talk*. The student could tell why he liked the book and, perhaps, read selected portions orally. An oral review of a book often will interest other students in reading the book.

Art can also be used as a culminating activity after a student has read a book. The student could illustrate a favorite scene in the book or make a mural showing selected events that occurred. He might construct a diorama showing a setting from the book. Another art-related activity would be for the student to design an illustrated book jacket for the book he read or create an advertisement to *sell* the book.

Drama can be used as an alternative to written book reports. Students can dress up as favorite characters and act out important events in books they have read. They can also create puppets of the key characters in a book and present a puppet show to their classmates.

For students who enjoy writing out a review of a book, a file could be kept to store such reviews. Students who wished to see what others thought of a particular book could consult the file to see if anyone wrote a review of it. Selected written book reviews could be posted periodically for use by students.

Students may enjoy rewriting a selected portion of a book, such as the ending. They might also enjoy rewriting a short book in the format of a play. Some students could make an audiotape of a short book to be listened to by other students.

A teacher should try to set aside time for students to read portions of favorite books aloud to her or to an older student, aide, or parent volunteer. Most students thoroughly enjoy reading privately to their teacher, and activities of this type make reading even more *special* for the student.

The book report alternatives mentioned thus far are all useful after a student completes a book. What about the student who does not want to finish a book he is reading? Occasionally, the situation will occur where a student selects a particular book and, after reading part of the book, finds that he totally dislikes it. The wise teacher will simply allow the student to record the number of pages read and then will assist him in selecting a more appropriate book. Being forced to finish a book he does not like could cause the student to dislike reading. At best, he will simply *put off* reading the book when he could be spending his time reading a book he liked.

Chapter 7 has discussed only a few of the many ways a teacher can develop reading interests and an appreciation of reading. Experienced teachers use a variety of techniques to excite their students about reading. Teachers whose students are *turned on* to reading are the real *reading experts*. New teachers might be wise to investigate their methods, for: "The role of teachers in stimulating voluntary reading among children and young people is . . . potentially the most powerful of all adult influences upon the young."[2]

POSTTEST

1. Elaborate on why reading aloud to students encourages them to engage in independent reading.

[2] *Promoting Voluntary Reading for Children and Young People* (Paris: UNESCO, 1980), p. 18.

2. Explain the use of an *interest inventory*.
3. Identify three sources of books for the classroom reading center.
4. Relate how television can have a positive effect on student reading.
5. Explain what is meant by *reading appreciation*.
6. Summarize the relationship between the physical environment of a classroom and a student's desire to engage in voluntary reading.
7. Identify the strongest motivating factor on student reading.
8. Describe how a *book display* can be used to promote reading as a leisure-time activity.
9. What is the best way to conduct competitions like *book contests*?
10. Describe four alternatives to written book reports.
11. Identify six types of books that can be included in the classroom collection.
12. Explain how the emotional climate of a classroom influences a student's interest in reading.

APPENDIX A

Interest Inventory for Primary Students

1. Name: ______________________________
2. Age: ______________________________
3. Birthdate: ______________________________
4. How many brothers do you have? ______________
5. How many sisters do you have? ______________
6. Do you live with both parents? ______________
7. Father's occupation: ______________________
8. Mother's occupation: ______________________
9. What would you like to be when you grow up? ____________
____
10. Have you ever been outside of your state? ____________
11. If yes, where did you go and what did you do? ____________
____
12. What are some of your favorite television shows? ____________
____

13. Do you have an allowance? ____________________
14. If yes, how do you spend it? ____________________
____
15. Do you have any chores that you do around your house? ______
16. If yes, what do you do? ____________________
____
17. Do you have a pet? ____________________
18. If yes, what is it? ____________________
19. What are some of your favorite books? ____________________
____
20. If someone gave you $1,000, what would you do with it?
____

APPENDIX B

Interest Inventory for Older Students

1. What is your name? ____________________
2. How old are you? ____________________
   When is your birthday? ____________________
3. How many brothers do you have? ____________________
   How many sisters do you have? ____________________
4. What type of work does your father do? ____________________
5. What type of work does your mother do? ____________________
6. Do you live with both of your parents? ____________________
7. What are your hobbies? ____________________
8. What is your favorite sport? ____________________
9. What is your favorite animal? ____________________
10. Do you have a pet? ____________________
    If yes, what is it? ____________________
11. Do you have a television set? ____________________
12. What is your favorite television show? ____________________
13. Do you ever go to the movies? ____________________
    If yes, name one you liked: ____________________
14. Who is your favorite actor or actress? ____________________
15. What kinds of books do you like? ____________________

16. What is your favorite book? ______
17. What books do you own? ______

______

18. Do you have an allowance? ______
19. Have you earned any money? ______ If yes, how? ______

______

20. What do you do with your money? ______

______

21. What would you like to do when you grow up? ______

______

22. What would your parents like you to do when you grow up?

______

23. Where would you like to go on vacation? ______
24. If someone gave you $500, what would you do with it?

______

25. If you could be anything or anyone, whom or what would you be? ______

Complete these sentences:

26. The thing I like best at school is ______.
27. If I could change my name, I would be ______.
28. I get angry when ______.
29. If I could have three wishes, I would wish for these:
    a. ______
    b. ______
    c. ______
30. The worst thing that ever happened to me was ______

______.

31. The best thing that ever happened to me was ______

______.

32. In this class I would like to ______

______.

FICTION

INDEX